What Your Donors Want

. . . *And Why!*

The Ultimate Guide to
Fundraising Communications

The cover for George Smith's 1996 book from White Lion Press. You might notice a similarity with the image on our cover: a dog asking for "help!" Guess what? Total coincidence.

I didn't own *Asking Properly*. Andrea Hopkins, my cover designer, had never seen the book. Our own line of thought had simply been: "Hey, pictures of puppies and kittens help raise money, right? Why not have the puppy itself asking for help? How irresistibly cute is that!"

Then, a few days before my book was to be printed, I ran across a tweet showing George's cover and thought, "[Expletive deleted.]"

So we chose to turn our cover coincidence into a tribute to the great George Smith, "guru, curmudgeon, humorist." You can (and should, if you're any kind of writer) order George's books from White Lion Press. Many articles by him are available for free on SOFII.org.

What Your Donors Want

. . . *And Why!*

The Ultimate Guide to Fundraising Communications

TOM AHERN

Emerson & Church, Publishers

First printed in August 2017

Printed in the United States of America

This text is printed on acid-free paper.

Copies of this book are available from the publisher at discount when purchased in quantity.

Emerson & Church, Publishers
15 Brook Street, Medfield, MA 02052
Tel. 508-359-0019
www.emersonandchurch.com

Library of Congress Cataloging-in-Publication Data

Names: Ahern, Tom, author.
Title: What your donors want . . . and why! : the ultimate guide to fundraising communications / Tom Ahern.
Description: Medfield, Massachusetts : Emerson & Church, Publishers, [2017]
Identifiers: LCCN 2017027353 | ISBN 9781889102627 (pbk. : alk. paper)
Subjects: LCSH: Fund raising. | Business communication. | Customer relations. | Nonprofit organizations.
Classification: LCC HG177 .A344 2017 | DDC 658.15/224—dc23 LC record available at https://lccn.loc.gov/2017027353

Dedication

Simone: Thanks to you, begun again

Contents

View from Orbit

View from 30,000 Feet

Wheels Down

Into the Weeds

View from Orbit

CHAPTER 1

Insert this into your job description

My dear fundraiser: you're in sales.

Whatever else your employer might expect of you, your *real* job is to SELL your worthy cause to interested individuals, foundations, and corporate sponsors. I say "interested" because the DIS-interested won't give you more than a nominal gift at best. Usually they give you nothing.

Which of course begs a question: Why *would* people be interested in your cause? And the short answer is: for their own reasons—some knowable, some guessable, and some entirely private. I'll expand on all that later. For now, though, let's return to my first point: **you're in sales**.

So, what exactly *is* "selling"?

Wikipedia: "Selling is offering to exchange an item of value for a different item." Let's break down that slightly awkward definition. There are three parts we need to understand.

- **Part one of the definition is the "offer to exchange."** Entry-level fundraisers soon hear, "What's the number one reason people give to charity?" Pause. *"Because they are asked!"* When you ask for a gift you are, technically speaking, making an offer. No offer? No sale. No ask? No gift. Bear in mind that the success of your fundraising program will depend heavily on the quality of your offers. We'll talk in depth about offers in a later chapter.

- **Part two of the definition is the "item of value."** In the for-profit world, "items of value" would be goods or services, things you might need or want: a hat or a haircut, a car for your commute or a taxi ride from the airport, groceries or lunch at a restaurant. Goods or services.

The "item of value" that most charities have to offer is emotional gratification (and the occasional T-shirt).

Now, at first glance, emotional gratification might not seem like much of an offer. It's not a *thing*. You can't hang it on the wall or in your closet. You can't eat it.

Yet we crave it. We seek emotional gratification desperately all our lives. Which affords it tremendous penetrating power. It is a, maybe *the*, chief motivator of human action. Ask any neuroscientist.

In truth, emotional gratification is where the for-profit and the nonprofit worlds converge: they both use it to sell.

- **Part three of the definition is exchanging that item of value for "a different item."** You promised me (the donor) I'd be doing something important if I contributed. Promised me I'd be making a difference if I helped. So now I'm trusting you and making my donation. My donation is the "different item" exchanged for your charity's item of value, which is emotional gratification.[1]

Since you're in sales, you have a customer

All of the above will seem pretty obvious. Still, it took me at least 15 years to put the pieces together to my own satisfaction. There was plenty of misdirection.

"Don't think of gifts as transactions." I heard that over and over . . . even though that's exactly what gifts *are*, at an objective level (see the definition of selling above).

Also: opinion fought science.

Well-meaning staff would argue: "We should stop using sad photos of poor kids to raise money. It's manipulative. We shouldn't exploit the same kids we're trying to help, for crying out loud!" Even though indisputable research found that sad photos reliably awakened empathy . . . and raised *far* more money than happy or neutral photos. (We'll talk about this disquieting debate in a later chapter.)

There was, most critically, a lack of understanding of what a donor *really* is.

You are a fundraiser. Which means you are in sales. Which in turn means you have a customer. And that customer is the donor, current and to come.

---

1 But not always money: many nonprofits also desperately need volunteers. In that case, the "different item" is the volunteer's time. Nonprofits can also benefit from increased social media exposure, "likes" and "shares." In that case, the "different item" is access to someone's circle of friends and colleagues.

CHAPTER 2

Job #1? Keeping your customer happy

Once you've attracted a new customer (i.e., a first-time donor), your #1 job is to keep that customer happy . . . happy enough, anyway, to continue trusting your organization and sometimes giving.

And that, sorry to say, is where fundraisers and their organizations generally fail. How do I know? Because donor retention at most charities is unimpressive, mediocre, wan, embarrassing and a professional disgrace, as surveys repeatedly show.

Running backwards

In America, by far the world's largest fundraising marketplace and proud to be named "the most generous country on earth,"[2] year after depressing year, something like 75% of any charity's first-time donors **do NOT make a second gift**.

Let us pause to mourn. And to consider those results in a commercial context:

- "75% of our first-time diners say they'll never eat in our restaurant again."
- "75% of our first-time shoppers will never set foot in our shoe store again."
- "75% of our first-time customers will never get their hair styled here again."

Would ordinary businesses with similar dismal numbers succeed?

No, they would not.

Yet those dismal numbers are exactly what nonprofit executives never question and somehow hope to grow on.

Chuck Longfield, senior VP and Chief Scientist at Blackbaud, reported the following all-too-typical numbers for Australian fundraising in 2013:

- 59% of mail-acquired donors did NOT make a second gift
- 75% of web/digitally-acquired donors didn't make a second gift
- 93% of event-acquired donors didn't make a second gift

2 2014, according to the Charities Aid Foundation; tied with Burma/Myanmar.

Or consider this: the 2015 Fundraising Effectiveness Project (FEP), sponsored by AFP and the Urban Institute, found that for every 100 *new* donors charities gained, they lost 103 *existing* donors.

If you were running a race with those numbers, you'd be running backwards. The FEP also found that only 19% of first-time donors were retained in 2014, down from 23% the year before.

This is a serious financial problem: a donor who gives to your charity just once probably costs you money. You're spending two bucks to raise a buck.

"Our nonprofit sector is bleeding to death," Ken Burnett rued, in his foreword to Roger Craver's 2014 book, *Retention Fundraising.* "We're hemorrhaging donors, losing support as fast as we find it, seemingly condemned forever to pay a fortune just to stand still." It's a severe financial headwind. Poor donor retention, with its debilitating impact on the bottom line, is one big reason charities can't invest in growth, talent, or new ideas. They just don't have the money.

How deep is the problem?

In 2015, in a sample of 1,200 US charities, only 1 in 5—the vast *minority*—retained half their first-time donors, according to Bloomerang, a software firm serving small- and medium-sized nonprofits.

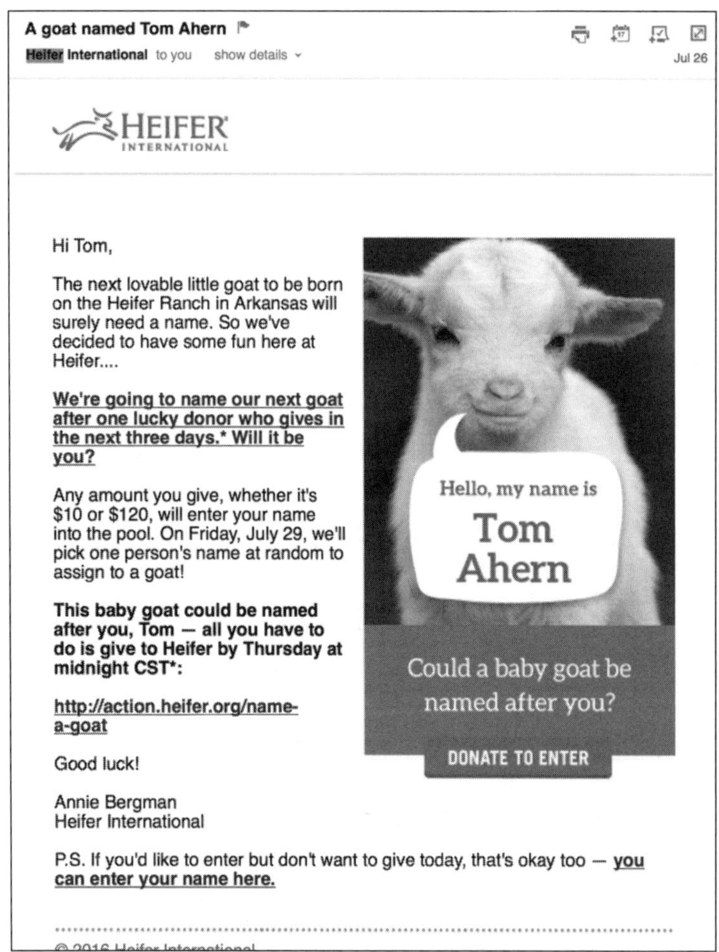

Years ago, I gave to Heifer; just once, but they stayed in touch. Recently I opened this Heifer email. Why? Because it hailed me with a personalized subject line, "A goat named Tom Ahern." I guess I was grateful it didn't say, "An old goat . . . ." I found myself happily donating $120 to buy a farm animal for a poor family overseas. I still think of that goat with pleasure.

CHAPTER 3

Donor, who art thou?

"A young donor in the U.S. is 60," Jeff Brooks noted in 2013.

Jeff writes direct mail for all sorts of national charities. He is one of the most successful and well-informed people working in fundraising today.

Jeff sent me a pie chart (see below) showing the ages of average American donors.[1] You might wonder: is this a typical breakdown by age? "It comes out this way no matter who does the research," Jeff told me. "I've seen it many times through the years."

Donors aged 65 and older comprise (by far) the largest slice of the American charity pie. Those under age 35 comprise the smallest slice of the same charity pie.

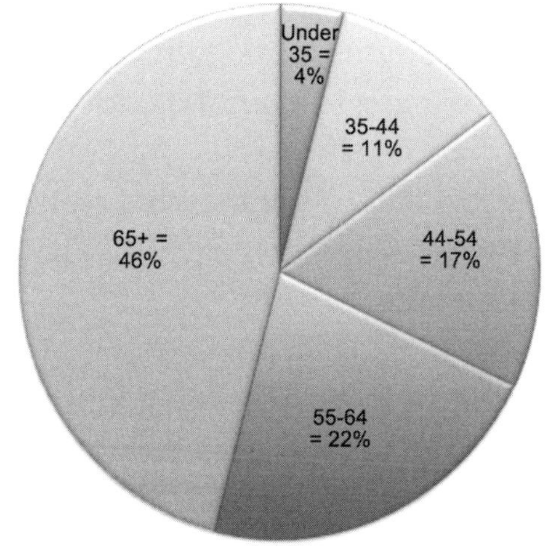

What you need to know: the young will likely always be the smallest slice of the charity pie in the United States, for predictable economic reasons.

Over his long career, Jeff Brooks has observed the following behavior: "At age 55, people start to become reliably charitable. They're starting to have some extra money." Their kids are through college. The house will be paid for soon. There is a bit of surplus money. "These households start to give to charity. And their giving

1 The chart originated with TrueSense, a major mail house, using data from Target Analytics Group, a Blackbaud company.

ramps up until age 65, where it plateaus. It continues from then on until something intervenes."

Something like illness, or destitution, or death. An animal welfare charity I know received its first check from a donor when the woman was age 55; her last gift came in when the woman was 101, just before she passed.

More evidence: I write the direct mail appeals for a major hospital group serving a metro population of more than 3 million. This hospital group has tens of thousands of donors. Since most were former patients, we know precisely how old they are. And the donor supporting this particular hospital group is on average 75 years old; not rounded up, not rounded down: exactly 75.

More evidence: in 2017, one of America's top 10 largest charities analyzed its vast donor database by age and shared that data with me. Its largest group of active donors was age 87. Its next largest group was age 86. After that came a tie: ages 85 and 75 had about the same number of active donors.

Is this reality holding your nonprofit back? You presume you're speaking to anyone of any age. Truth is, you're mostly speaking to older folks. And you're not saying what they need and want to hear.

Consequences of an older audience

Around 2012 the AIGA (essentially, the graphics designers' trade group in the United States) issued an advisory: "For eyes over 60, use 14 point type for body copy."

Lest we forget: a good "customer service experience" is one of the chief reasons why donors stick with you. For eyes of "a certain age," 14 point type will be a good customer service experience . . . while 12 point type will not be.

But type size is the least of it.

According to geriatric psychologist David Solie, the elderly are on "a journey" that's unrecognized by most, including their children and professional caregivers. "Many of us look at members of our parents' generation and see a diminished version of the vibrant people we once knew," he writes in his book, *How to Say It to Seniors.*[2] "Surely they aren't developing anymore, because we can see them declining right before our eyes."

But that's not true. They *are* developing.

They are working their way through what Solie calls "their end-of-life tasks." These tasks include "searching for a legacy."

---

2 David Solie, *How to Say It to Seniors: Closing the Communication Gap with Our Elders* (New York: Prentice Hall Press, 2004).

Solie also calls it "life review." And it is essential and involuntary. "Every day, every hour, whether they mention it or not, the seventy-plus age group is reviewing their lives."

I mention this because it's a stage of life mostly unsuspected, until you get there yourself. Yet think how important acts of charity can be to someone putting the final touches on her legacy.

Acts of charity help define us. Those acts say, "This is in part who I am. This is what I do for others. This is how I try to help. This is me at my best and least selfish."

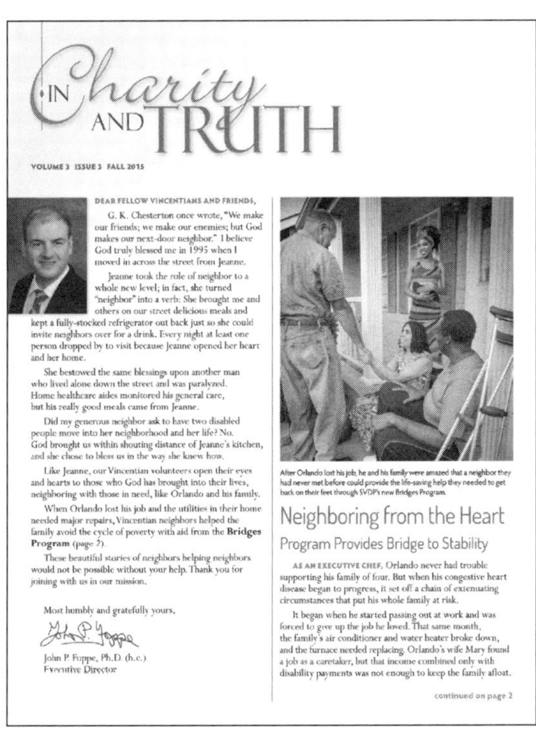

IN Charity AND TRUTH

VOLUME 3 ISSUE 3 FALL 2015

DEAR FELLOW VINCENTIANS AND FRIENDS,

G. K. Chesterton once wrote, "We make our friends; we make our enemies; but God makes our next-door neighbor." I believe God truly blessed me in 1995 when I moved in across the street from Jeanne.

Jeanne took the role of neighbor to a whole new level; in fact, she turned "neighbor" into a verb: She brought me and others on our street delicious meals and kept a fully-stocked refrigerator out back just so she could invite neighbors over for a drink. Every night at least one person dropped by to visit because Jeanne opened her heart and her home.

She bestowed the same blessings upon another man who lived alone down the street and was paralyzed. Home healthcare aides monitored his general care, but his really good meals came from Jeanne.

Did my generous neighbor ask to have two disabled people move into her neighborhood and her life? No. God brought us within shouting distance of Jeanne's kitchen, and she chose to bless us in the way she knew how.

Like Jeanne, our Vincentian volunteers open their eyes and hearts to those who God has brought into their lives, neighboring with those in need, like Orlando and his family.

When Orlando lost his job and the utilities in their home needed major repairs, Vincentian neighbors helped the family avoid the cycle of poverty with aid from the **Bridges Program** (page 2).

These beautiful stories of neighbors helping neighbors would not be possible without your help. Thank you for joining with us in our mission.

Most humbly and gratefully yours,

John P. Foppe, Ph.D. (h.c.)
Executive Director

After Orlando lost his job, he and his family were amazed that a neighbor they had never met before could provide the life-saving help they needed to get back on their feet through SVDP's new Bridges Program.

Neighboring from the Heart

Program Provides Bridge to Stability

AS AN EXECUTIVE CHEF, Orlando never had trouble supporting his family of four. But when his congestive heart disease began to progress, it set off a chain of extenuating circumstances that put his whole family at risk.

It began when he started passing out at work and was forced to give up the job he loved. That same month, the family's air conditioner and water heater broke down, and the furnace needed replacing. Orlando's wife Mary found a job as a caretaker, but that income combined only with disability payments was not enough to keep the family afloat.

continued on page 2

Anne Kirwan, director of development at the Society of St. Vincent de Paul, Archdiocesan Council of St. Louis, reported a 317% increase in contributions year over year when it changed its look and began focusing on donor-centricity. The old cover focused on what the programs did. The new cover focused on what the donor did.

There are plenty of younger donors. But . . .

You can acquire younger donors in bulk through something called "face to face" (F2F) fundraising. It occurs on the streets, not in the mailbox nor online.

Personable, energetic, well-trained and licensed 20- and 30-somethings intercept on the street other 20- and 30-somethings (or, if the pickings are slim, older people), to sign them up for monthly donations, usually to a brand-name, trusted charity such as Oxfam.

F2F fundraising originated in the UK in the late 20th century, with Greenpeace among its leaders. The tactic became so widespread (and intrusive) on certain London streets that by 2002 it had earned a common nickname in the press: "chugging," short for "charity mugging."

Chugging may offend the man on the street, but it works. Gifts obtained through F2F now amount to one-third of Australia's annual charitable haul, little more than a decade after the tactic arrived on its shores. F2F crews sign up hundreds of thousands of new donors every year.

And yet . . . even in Australia, where F2F fundraising is huge . . . older donors rule the roost.

After crunching the numbers, Sean Triner, co-founder of Pareto, that country's largest direct mail and phone fundraising agency, concluded simply: "Older donors are better." He meant F2F donors aged 40 and up. Why? They tend to stick longer and hence give more in total.

"The younger groups will NOT stay with you in good numbers," Jeff Brooks noted, "even if you can find them. But the 'almost old' are promising. They give higher average gifts than 65+, and once they're aboard, they can stay with you for many years. This is the group that can turn around your fortunes and drive you to a brighter future."

The next big "giving generation" will be baby boomers, born between 1946 and 1964. In 2016, the oldest were 70, the youngest were 52. You won't see the last of them until 2064 or so. Together, baby boomers control over 80% of personal financial assets in the United States, says a well-sourced Wikipedia article.

CHAPTER 4

Lifetime value (LTV)

- **The lifetime value (LTV)[1] of someone who gives just once to your cause will be no higher than $35, likely.** Fifty dollars is an above-average entry-level gift for most charities in English-speaking countries. Typically, your organization will *lose* money trying to acquire first-time donors.

  Though your boss might not like to hear it, it is perfectly normal to lose money bringing in a new donor. It's an investment in your charity's future to spend $2 to acquire $1 in newbie giving. Every charity suffers donor attrition every year. A "new donor acquisition program" is a must.

  Charities get off cheap.

  They spend just $50 or so to acquire each new donor, one expert estimates. Starbucks, on the other hand, spends $1,400 in advertising to acquire one new customer. "You'd say Starbucks is foolish," Roger Craver wrote, "until you learned that the 20 year Lifetime Value of a Starbucks customer is $14,099."[2] New donors are cheap by comparison.

- If that "newly acquired $50 donor" continues to give to your cause the same amount annually for 10 years (which, in truth, would be a rare occurrence), **her LTV will grow to something like $500 total**. Still, in the end, you'll be in the black many times over with that particular donor. In fact, you probably went into the black somewhere between her second and third gifts.

- Now, if that same new donor soon coverts to monthly giving at $10/month (because you've phoned her to ask for the upgrade) AND continues giving

---

1 In *Fundraising Principles and Practice* (Jossey-Bass, 2010), Dr. Adrian Sargeant and co-author Dr. Jen Shang, suggest lifetime value (LTV) as a good way to set fundraising priorities and keep acquisition costs under control. Do you really need to add a 5K charity run, for instance? "Charities can employ an LTV analysis to increase their overall profitability by getting rid of (or never recruiting) donors who will never be profitable and by concentrating resources on recruiting and retaining those who will."

2 *The Agitator*, Oct. 17, 2012.

monthly for 10 years (you'll have to renew her credit card from time to time) . . . well, **her LTV rises to around $1,200 cumulatively**.

- If that same donor has the means *and* you persuade her eventually to give $1,000 yearly instead of $50 yearly, **her 10-year LTV might approach $9,000 ultimately**. (And, yes, many of your future major donors will enter as modest donors initially.[3])
- And if that very same donor identifies so strongly with your cause that she continues giving for years . . . AND also—saints be praised and hand out the halos!—she decides to add your charity to her will . . . well, her LTV, as realized at probate, will likely soar **to something like $50,000 or more** (*far* more, often enough).

So, which lifetime value (LTV) is most worth your focus, your resources, and a plan to achieve specific goals?

- $50
- $500
- $1,200
- $9,000
- $50,000

Obvious, right?

Looked at through the LTV lens, the priorities become (1) monthly giving, (2) moving mid-range donors upward into major gift territory, and (3) successfully promoting charitable bequests.

3 Jerry Panas reported in 2017, "When Harvard did a study after their last campaign, of their 254 million-dollar donors, two out of three started with first-time gifts of $100 or less." And it's not just Harvard: the phenomenon is common across the charity world.

View from 30,000 Feet

CHAPTER 5

How to improve first-time donor retention

You can't expect 100% retention of new donors.

Every year, deaths and other ordinary attritions (career moves, life changes like retirement) chip away at your donor and prospect database.

But you *can* shoot far higher than 20% retention of first-time donors. Jeff Brooks says, "A properly-run fundraising program should retain somewhere between 30 to 50 percent of its first-time donors." One public radio station in the United States regularly attains 90% retention of new donors! Of course, public radio has an advantage: it provides a welcome service (great programming) to its avid "listener supporters." There is a built-in, intimate relationship at play.

Still, improving your donor retention by 10%, 20% or more should be easy enough, if you accept (as I do) Stephen Pidgeon's advice.

What Stephen said

Stephen Pidgeon built and eventually sold a major UK direct mail fundraising agency, Tangible. In his 2015 "everything I know" advice book, *How to Love Your Donors (to Death)*, he makes this point: "It is the fundraiser's job, your only job, to make the supporter feel good about supporting your charity. You have to love your donors. The money will follow."

Get out your highlighter and mark Stephen's words. While you're at it, highlight these words by Mark Phillips, too, written in October 2015:

"The only thing that matters a damn is the donor experience. If we'd got that right, we'd have never been in this situation. I still don't understand why so many organisations dropped fundraising for brand awareness and an addiction to interruption recruitment techniques. The result is that we have a massive pool of people who—at best—tolerate how fundraisers treat them." Mark is founder (1997) and managing director of Bluefrog, an award-winning London-based creative agency serving many of the UK's top-performing charities.

The math: A formula for calculating retention rate

From Roger Craver's essential book, *Retention Fundraising:*

- Step 1: Count the total number of donors who gave in your most recent calendar or fiscal year.
- Step 2: Divide the number of donors who made a donation in year 2 by the total in Step 1.
- Step 3: Multiply the result from Step 2 by 100 to obtain your retention rate as a percentage.

CHAPTER 6

Why bequests are your organization's easiest road to riches

First, Stephen Pidgeon . . . .

He devotes a chapter of his delightfully frank book to the topic of "legacy marketing"; i.e., why every charity should vigorously promote charitable bequests. As he points out:

> The sums involved [in legacy marketing] are so huge, the impact of this money is so transforming, that it transcends any other form of fundraising.
>
> All but the biggest major gifts are chicken feed in comparison to legacies. Regular monthly gifts paid through the bank? Legacies dwarf even this welcome source of money. Corporate gifts are but pennies in a bucket.
>
> Yet people in charities (not, thankfully, the fundraisers) don't take legacy marketing seriously at all.
>
> Many trustees and senior charity staff believe legacies are the gift of the legacy fairies, they are that complacent. They love the money flowing in but don't seem to think the flow can be promoted nor that it might stop one day without such promotion.

Here's why it's easy

The following bit of vital research appears in *Iceberg Philanthropy*. It's part of the profile of "Jacqueline," the "average" North American donor discussed in great detail and depth by this remarkable book.

"Jacqueline is typical of those donors who send your organization $35 cheques through the mail. She's the classic ordinary donor. . . . Your major gift officer pays no attention to donors like Jacqueline. Nor does your planned giving officer."[1]

1 Fraser Green, Ruth McDonald, and Jose Van Herpt, *Iceberg Philanthropy: Unlocking Extraordinary Gifts from Ordinary Donors* (Ottawa: FLA Group, 2007), p. 77.

The fact that Jacqueline remains invisible to most nonprofit organizations, even though "she might well have been giving to you consistently for 10 or 20 years," means, as *Iceberg Philanthropy* hammers home, that you're probably ignoring most of your best prospects for a bequest.

As Good Works, a fundraising consultancy in Canada, advises, "Legacy marketing . . . is about getting a small number of very large gifts from your 'average' donors. These are the donors who aren't on your radar screen already, who aren't interested in tea and banana bread with a planned giving officer, but who are very loyal to your cause."

In other words, **you already know who your best bequest prospects are**. They're the donors in your database who give to you faithfully. They're the donors in your database who give you larger than average gifts each year.

You just have to overcome one simple obstacle. Asked why they haven't yet put a gift in their wills, loyal donors commonly say, "It just never occurred to me."

Make sure it occurs to them

Once a year, mail your best bequest prospects a brief letter, reminding them that they can make a spectacular difference by adding a gift to your charity in their wills.

According to "Dr. Death," a moniker used by bequest expert Richard Radcliffe, that single extra letter each year is a basic requirement. If you're not already sending out that annual letter to your best bequest prospects, you do not yet have a solid bequest marketing program.

What's in the letter? Here's a basic model:

- Start by **thanking** your donor deeply . . . humbly . . . for her years of generosity. Remind her how important her charity has been to the success of the mission.
- Don't beat around the bush, but don't come right out and ask for a gift. Ask for her **consideration**, instead. "Next time you review your estate plans, would you please consider adding a gift of any size to your will?"
- Let her know about your charity's **legacy society** (if you don't have one, start one). "If you do someday choose to put a gift in your will, I hope you'll let me know. I'd love to enroll you in a very special group of wonderful, forward-thinking people like you whom we call our Best Friends Forever."

- In conclusion, **thank** her some more.
- PS: **Offer free information** about charitable bequests. "We have this free, informative, plain-language booklet that explains everything. You'll meet some other people who will explain why they're glad they've added charity to their estate plans."

Talk about it a lot

Charities grow tongue-tied and cautious around the topic of death. There's a remedy for that condition: *stop thinking of your bequestors as dead people.*

Here is Richard Radcliffe's favorite saying; in a workshop, he'll say it a dozen times: "Bequests are life driven, death activated."

My wife and I wrote our first will in our young 40s, as many newly married couples do. We included charitable bequests in that original will and in every update since.

"Today's donors want what they've always wanted—to act on their values, to express compassion, to be part of something bigger, to feel better about themselves, to have an impact and make a difference, to respond to fear, to be appreciated. Motives and needs like these haven't changed and never will," as Tom Belford wrote in The Agitator in 2016.

Bear in mind that the writing and rewriting of wills is "prompted by life events—death, birth, marriage, health, travel, retirement," as Jeff Comfort, VP of principal gifts and gift planning at the Oregon State University Foundation, has stated. "That's why it's so important to have a regular cadence of marketing messages. Drip, drip, drip. Because you never know when the time might be right."

Adding Charity to Your Will or IRA

A quick guide to the pleasure and promise of charitable bequests

Hampton Roads Community Foundation

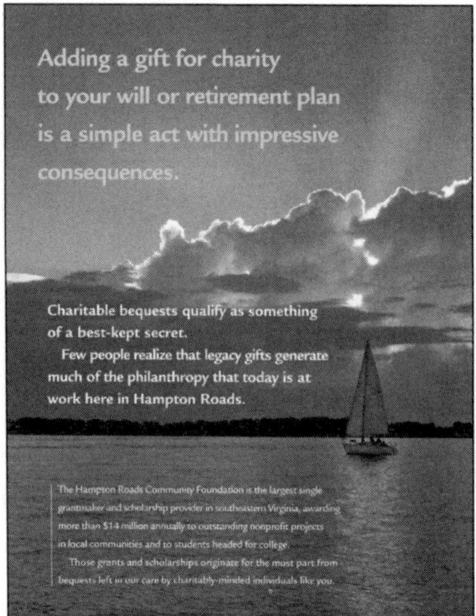

Adding a gift for charity to your will or retirement plan is a simple act with impressive consequences.

Charitable bequests qualify as something of a best-kept secret.

Few people realize that legacy gifts generate much of the philanthropy that today is at work here in Hampton Roads.

The Hampton Roads Community Foundation is the largest single grantmaker and scholarship provider in southeastern Virginia, awarding more than $14 million annually to outstanding nonprofit projects in local communities and to students headed for college.

Those grants and scholarships originate for the most part from bequests left in our care by charitably-minded individuals like you.

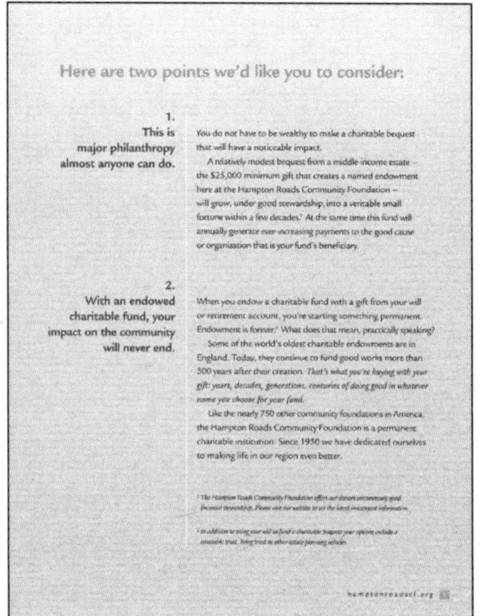

Here are two points we'd like you to consider:

1. This is major philanthropy almost anyone can do.

You do not have to be wealthy to make a charitable bequest that will have a noticeable impact.

A relatively modest bequest from a middle-income estate – the $25,000 minimum gift that creates a named endowment here at the Hampton Roads Community Foundation – will grow, under good stewardship, into a veritable small fortune within a few decades.[1] At the same time this fund will annually generate ever-increasing payments to the good cause or organization that is your fund's beneficiary.

2. With an endowed charitable fund, your impact on the community will never end.

When you endow a charitable fund with a gift from your will or retirement account, you're starting something permanent. Endowment is forever.[2] What does that mean, practically speaking?

Some of the world's oldest charitable endowments are in England. Today, they continue to fund good works more than 500 years after their creation. *That's what you're buying with your gift: years, decades, generations, centuries of doing good in whatever name you choose for your fund.*

Like the nearly 750 other community foundations in America, the Hampton Roads Community Foundation is a permanent charitable institution. Since 1950 we have dedicated ourselves to making life in our region even better.

hamptonroadscf.org

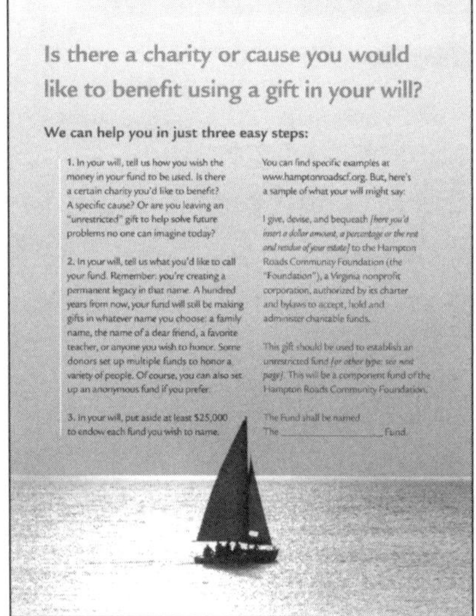

Is there a charity or cause you would like to benefit using a gift in your will?

We can help you in just three easy steps:

1. In your will, tell us how you wish the money in your fund to be used. Is there a certain charity you'd like to benefit? A specific cause? Or are you leaving an "unrestricted" gift to help solve future problems no one can imagine today?

2. In your will, tell us what you'd like to call your fund. Remember: you're creating a permanent legacy in that name. A hundred years from now, your fund will still be making gifts in whatever name you choose: a family name, the name of a dear friend, a favorite teacher, or anyone you wish to honor. Some donors set up multiple funds to honor a variety of people. Of course, you can also set up an anonymous fund if you prefer.

3. In your will, put aside at least $25,000 to endow each fund you wish to name.

You can find specific examples at www.hamptonroadscf.org. But, here's a sample of what your will might say:

I give, devise, and bequeath *[here you'd insert a dollar amount, a percentage or the rest and residue of your estate]* to the Hampton Roads Community Foundation (the "Foundation"), a Virginia nonprofit corporation, authorized by its charter and bylaws to accept, hold and administer charitable funds.

This gift should be used to establish an unrestricted fund *[or other type: see next page]*. This will be a component fund of the Hampton Roads Community Foundation.

The Fund shall be named The ______________ Fund.

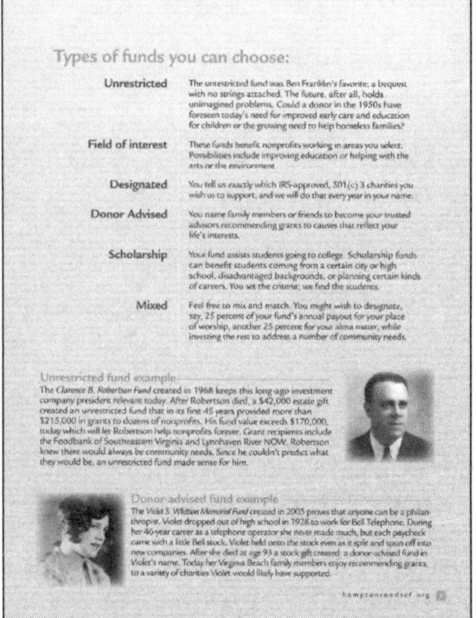

Types of funds you can choose:

Unrestricted The unrestricted fund was Ben Franklin's favorite: a bequest with no strings attached. The future, after all, holds unimagined problems. Could a donor in the 1950s have foreseen today's need for improved early care and education for children or the growing need to help homeless families?

Field of interest These funds benefit nonprofits working in areas you select. Possibilities include improving education or helping with the arts or the environment.

Designated You tell us exactly which IRS-approved, 501(c) 3 charities you wish us to support, and we will do that every year in your name.

Donor Advised You name family members or friends to become your trusted advisors recommending grants to causes that reflect your life's interests.

Scholarship Your fund assists students going to college. Scholarship funds can benefit students coming from a certain city or high school, disadvantaged backgrounds, or planning certain kinds of careers. You set the criteria; we find the students.

Mixed Feel free to mix and match. You might wish to designate, say, 25 percent of your fund's annual payout for your place of worship, another 25 percent for your alma mater, while investing the rest to address a number of community needs.

Unrestricted fund example

The *Clarence B. Robertson Fund* created in 1968 keeps this long-ago investment company president relevant today. After Robertson died, a $42,000 estate gift created an unrestricted fund that in its first 45 years provided more than $215,000 in grants to dozens of nonprofits. His fund value exceeds $170,000, today which will let Robertson help nonprofits forever. Grant recipients include the Foodbank of Southeastern Virginia and Lynnhaven River NOW. Robertson knew there would always be community needs. Since he couldn't predict what they would be, an unrestricted fund made sense for him.

Donor-advised fund example

The *Violet S. Whitten Memorial Fund* created in 2005 proves that anyone can be a philanthropist. Violet dropped out of high school in 1928 to work for Bell Telephone. During her 46-year career as a telephone operator she never made much, but each paycheck came with a little Bell stock. Violet held onto the stock even as it split and spun off into new companies. After she died at age 93 a stock gift created a donor-advised fund in Violet's name. Today her Virginia Beach family members enjoy recommending grants to a variety of charities Violet would likely have supported.

hamptonroadscf.org

In 2009, Virginia's Hampton Roads Community Foundation began promoting endowed funds to the general community, offering a plain-English, non-technical "quick guide to the pleasure and promise of charitable bequests." The foundation experimented with all sorts of advertising channels, even billboards, budgeting something like $55,000 for the launch. In the end, the most effective ads proved to be 15-second sponsor spots on local National Public Radio, featuring a custom URL: leaveabequest.org. The return on the foundation's initial investment has been handsome: within a few years, the number of pledgers enrolled in the legacy society doubled. Reproduced here: the cover and opening two spreads from the 2014 second printing of the guide.

CHAPTER 7

You know who is *not* your customer? Your boss and board

Subpar retention is an easy enough problem to fix, if you focus on your donors and their emotional needs.

But there's a lurking enemy that prevents many fundraisers from doing their best work.

Ignorance regarding how to properly communicate with donors is firmly rooted in the nonprofit world, especially at the approval level, among bosses and the board. Do any of these true-life situations sound familiar?

- "My boss insists on writing all the appeals himself. And he's boring!"
- "The archdiocese says we shouldn't spend money on a newsletter because it shows poor stewardship of donor resources."
- "My boss says our donors are unique, so normal rules don't apply."
- "My boss told me to switch to emailed newsletters exclusively because nobody reads print anymore."
- "My headmaster won't let me use a P.S. in an appeal. He says it's undignified."
- "My boss heard me out. Then he told me, and I quote, 'Sorry. That's not how we do things here.' At least he said he was sorry."
- "My board chair insisted I take out the indents. He thinks they're un-businesslike."
- "The board chair said he never reads anything longer than a one-page letter, so that's what he insists on."

I have a rule. I call it the Verbatim Rule. I will not accept any new direct mail client unless they promise to mail what I write *without changing a word* (except to correct factual errors, of course).

The Verbatim Rule protects my clients from their native urge to rewrite. Being literate does not make you a competent direct mail writer. Nor does receiving a daily handful of uninvited direct mail appeals, most of which you throw away unexamined. Believing otherwise is akin to assuming you could win an Olympic race because you happen to have two legs.

On the other hand, I've studied and practiced direct mail writing for 20 years and have a track record of decent results. What I think about direct mail matters. What the untrained think on that particular and complicated topic does not. In fact, uninformed opinions in direct mail are very dangerous. It's a sensitive, expensive medium. It's easy to fail completely. It's very, very hard to succeed.

And yet . . .

If I had a penny for every fundraiser who's approached me after a workshop to complain about her boss second-guessing her direct mail appeals, I'd own a penthouse in Paris.

If your goal is to please your boss, your board chair, or fellow staff, you might as well close this book right now. My forecast: you will struggle to succeed in donor communications.

Your boss, board, and fellow staff are NOT your target audiences. Though they often presume to judge and fiddle with your work, in the end their likes and dislikes are irrelevant to your charity's fundraising success.

You might hold onto your job by kowtowing to their ignorance. But you're unlikely to wildly succeed in job #1: satisfying your "donor customer."

Highlight the following two paragraphs:

In donor communications, untrained opinions are not only worthless, they're dangerous to your nonprofit's bottom line.

In a professionally run operation, the chief fundraiser will have full, autonomous control over all donor communications, print and digital: appeals, thanks, newsletters, donation landing pages on the website, social media, multichannel campaigns, whatever.

After all, it's your neck on the line if your stuff doesn't work; not theirs. I'll always remember the board chair who proclaimed with a superior sniff, "We tried direct mail. It didn't work for us." Which really only means they sent out a badly written appeal, probably to the wrong households, and reaped (predictably) nothing.

Non-professionals use the wrong criteria

Inventor Henry Ford once observed, "If we'd asked the public what they wanted, they would have said, 'faster horses.'"

People work with what they know. Ask an untrained person for an opinion, and you'll get one, particularly if it's about the written word. But the context and references on which that opinion is based will be personal, not professional.

When an untrained person says, "I like it," it's a matter of inexperienced, personal taste.

When a trained person says, "I like it," it's a matter of judgment, using recognized and proven criteria.

In a professional approval process, personal taste is irrelevant and often misleading because it tends to favor the safe over the bold. It's risk averse.

BIG mistake.

Advertising legend David Ogilvy, wrote, "You cannot *bore* people into buying your product; you can only *interest* them in buying it."

Ask any good marketer: Bold outsells bland every time. And that goes for fundraising, too. In the bowels of the direct mail industry, there's a belief that if no one complains, you probably haven't pushed hard enough. Someone should call to give you an earful: "I just got your latest fundraising appeal. How dare you show a picture like that!"

Communications committees are a bad idea

The "communications committee"—that time-honored confection of clueless boards—just multiplies the problem.

Instead of a single untrained opinion making uninformed decisions, now you have several, working together gamely but lamely. Fundraisers with training (and a sprig of pride) will avoid such committees like the plague (unless they can control and use them for other ends). In his classic *Confessions of an Advertising Man*, Ogilvy reminds us of this apt rhyme:

Search all the parks in all your cities;
You'll find no statues of committees.

If your charity requires its chief fundraiser to seek approval from a communications committee, abolish that practice immediately (unless by the rarest of good fortune your committee happens to be made up of direct mail professionals).

Fundraisers cannot succeed when collective ignorance has the final say.

000002

101 East Fifth Street, Suite 2000 ■ Saint Paul, MN 55101 ■ 651-222-2193

"Will you be my friend?"

Dear Robert Richter,

That's *your* very own Mississippi River talking.

Actually, that's the Mississippi *pleading* ... for your help.

You see, a river can't fix itself. But you *can* ... if you choose to become a *Friend of the Mississippi River*.

FMR = Friends of the Mississippi River. We're only missing one thing: **you**.

I want you to join FMR.

You'll feel proud of your membership in this special family of nature lovers!

And I ask you: *What could be better* than becoming best friends with that big, legendary, world-renowned, sung-about, vital, despoiled-but-fighting-back river running through your own backyard?

The Mississippi River is Minnesota's responsibility.

It originates as a humble stream at a small woodland lake in our state. And it gets its first full taste of what humans can do to abuse a waterway when it hits the Twin Cities, where, for well over a century it served as an industrial sewer, made utterly devoid of life.

With your help, we can heal that abuse.

fmr.org

First page of a six-page letter for a donor acquisition campaign was written under the Verbatim Rule. There are a dozen different persuasion tactics laboring behind the scenes: everything from anthropomorphism to emotional workhorses like fear and anger to a matching gift offer. The first protest from an untrained committee would have likely been, "Who the heck's going to read a six-page letter?!?" So, how did the letter fare? Response far exceeded industry standards. In a single mailing, St. Paul-based Friends of the Mississippi River increased its membership by 17.6%, attracting strong response from like-minded individuals in Minnesota who'd given in the past to the National Audubon Society, The Nature Conservancy, the Sierra Club and other environmental defenders.

CHAPTER 8

Are your expectations realistic?

How long will the average donor stay with a charity?

I asked my global family of top experts this simplistic question: "How long, do you think, the average donor gives to the same charity? Five years? Ten years? Twenty-five years? Off the top of your head."

I learned one thing right away: don't overestimate the "stickiness" of new donors.

Over half of first-time donors give just once, several respondents pointed out. Very few donors stay longer than a few years: precisely 4.6 years in the UK, according to Dr. Adrian Sargeant's research, based on an analysis of 5 million records. "It's an amalgam of all forms of giving, so it lumps together very different types of giving," he admitted. "But as a number, it's nice. And it's getting lower each year."

Which means a program for regularly acquiring new donors remains vital to your nonprofit's financial health.

Degrees of separation vs. intimacy

Beth Ann Locke said this: "The rise of peer-to-peer giving"—e.g., I sponsor you in a 10K run—"shortens the lifespan of donors. They give to a 'charity' but are usually only giving to their friends. This certainly has the great opportunity of casting a wide net, but the net is gossamer."

Remember her comment as you read Mark Phillips's response (he's the founder and manager of Bluefrog in London): "I find that the best 5% of the file tend to stick with you forever. The problem is the other 70% of people who only ever intended to give once. They really drag your average down."

Roger Craver, co-editor of The Agitator, and one of America's all-time direct mail champs, estimated donors stick around ". . . about 4 to 5 years, top of my head. The single donors who only ever give one gift weigh down longevity [as Mark said]. If you're looking only at donors who make two or more gifts, I would say the span is closer to 7 or 8 years."

Nor are all charities equally compelling. "When I had my heart attack, my local hospital fixed me right up" is an event to remember annually with a gift, if the hospital asks. Going out to a charity event is fun but ephemeral.

Rory Green, Associate Director of Advancement, faculty of Applied Sciences, Simon Fraser University: "Many of my donors have given consecutively for 10+ years . . . BUT we're a bit of an anomaly. I would imagine the answer would differ, too, across generations: [older people] longer and less so as donors get younger."

Beth Ann agreed: "I think older donors are more loyal. [At one hospital, there were] donors who had had hips and knees replaced who just gave and gave, as long as you kept asking, for 20+ years. I'd say with some universities it is the same, once the habit takes hold." In contrast, she witnessed a different pattern at an art museum: "You would bring them into the fold as donors after being members. Then they would fall off in a few years."

How many charities per donor per year?

Research published in *Iceberg Philanthopy*[1] found that almost half of Canadian direct mail donors, gave to between 6 and 10 charities a year. More than a third of respondents reported giving to more than 20 charities in a year. The US philanthropic marketplace is similar.

Here's the take-away: you share *your* "average donor" with a lot of other charities. You do not have an exclusive. And every year, new charities come knocking on your donor's door, begging for support. The number of charities in the United States has almost doubled over the past 15 years.

How can you compete successfully? Be very good at things other charities are generally poor at: thanking and reporting.

Does online giving dominate yet?

The Chronicle of Philanthropy asked America's 400 largest charities for data about their online fundraising results during 2013. What was learned?

"While online fundraising continues to gain steam, " the *Chronicle* reported,[2] "it still accounts for a very small portion of the money charities rely on. Among the 76 nonprofits that provided both their online and overall giving totals for 2013, the median share of online gifts is just 2 percent of all donations from private sources."

You can take comfort perhaps, if your nonprofit is not yet seeing big results from online giving, you're not alone.

But the trend is clear. "Online Giving Reaches Record High in 2016," trumpeted a Blackbaud report, released in February 2017. A record, yes, but pay attention: in 2016, online giving was

---

1 Fraser Green, Ruth McDonald, and Jose Van Herpt, *Iceberg Philanthropy: Unlocking Extraordinary Gifts from Ordinary Donors* (Ottawa: FLA Group, 2007), p. 81.

2 Alex Daniels and Anu Narayanswamy, "Online Giving Grows More Sophisticated," *Chronicle of Philanthropy*, May 18, 2014.

still just 7.2% of *all* giving across the United States. And it was only up a smidge from the previous year, when online accounted for 7.1% of the giving pie.

The digital environment's getting busier and tougher to succeed in. Did you know that in 2016 it took 2,000 fundraising emails "to generate a single gift"?[3]

One important thing to remember about online giving is this: *it's just another channel for connecting donors to your cause.*

These days, offline and online cooperate. Customer behavior will always gravitate toward convenience. By one estimate, about 20% of the gifts *prompted* by direct mail now are actually completed *online,* because people find the online experience easier than writing a check.

3 M+R, *Benchmarks 2017*, April 25, 2017: [number]

CHAPTER 9

Donor-centricity: the only secret I know to increased giving

What sort of improvement in revenue can your charity expect if it takes the small risk of talking to donors in a different way?

Here are some recent reports received from the front lines:

- "Our online donations doubled this year!"
- "366% uptick in giving."
- "Donations linked to the newsletter increased 50%."
- "Donations linked to the newsletter increased 150%."
- "In just four years, our legacy society doubled in size."
- "Our best year ever."

What do all these enviable leaps in income have in common?

Just one thing: all these fundraisers adopted "donor centricity" as the central focus of their communications.

In January 2014, I received a note from Angel Aloma, executive director of Food for the Poor, a Florida-based, faith-based aid charity with $1+ billion in annual income: "I want to reiterate that much of what we are doing now in regards to donor centricity was inspired by your wonderful presentation at the IFC [International Fundraising Congress, held annually in the Netherlands]. I am convinced that the reason why we have grown in the last years of tough economic conditions in the country is because of that wonderful switch that you inspired."

Thank you, Angel! Yet the real credit goes . . .

- . . . to you and your organization . . . for enacting the switch, from what you *were* doing to what you *are* doing (FYI, readers: changing is likely to be the hardest part of your journey);

This artwork, commissioned by the Better Fundraising Co., captures the essence of donor-centricity. Translated into other words: "With your help, we can do amazing good deeds. And without your help, those amazing good deeds just aren't possible."

- . . . to pioneers like Ken Burnett, who published his visionary *Relationship Fundraising* in 1992;
- . . . to Dr. Adrian Sargeant, Dr. Jen Shang and their scholarly co-conspirators, who took the sharp shears of science to a fundraising profession overgrown with conventional wisdom;
- . . . to all the *commercial* marketers who at least 60 years ago realized that "customer centricity" would be the best road to awesome financial growth . . . and hence paved the way.

Why people donate

"The story's about the donor," Seth Godin says.

Seth Godin is a Stanford MBA, a successful serial entrepreneur, and the best-selling author of more than a dozen mind-bending marketing books. Of the many guru bloggers I follow, he is the most consistently useful. His insights into consumer behavior are sharp and actionable, especially where donors are concerned.

"Every time someone donates to a good cause," Godin points out, "they're buying a story, a story that's worth more than the amount they donated." There is more treasure hidden in that observation than in King Solomon's lost mines. Godin goes on: "It might be the story of doing the right thing, or fitting in, or pleasing a friend or honoring a memory, but the story has value. For many, it's the story of what it means to be part of a community."

Notice two points:

1. donors play a role in the story they're buying, and
2. the purchased story is worth the money because it reinforces the donor's self-image: "I am a good person because I chipped in."

When a person makes a gift to charity, he's proving something to himself (and maybe others): *This is the kind of person I am.* Every gift to charity has the potential to extend a person's story in a meaningful and positive direction.

In her research, Jen Shang, a psychologist who studies philanthropic behavior, found that Americans describe a "good person" with nine favored adjectives: *caring*, *compassionate*, *fair*, *friendly*, *generous*, *hard-working*, *helpful*, *honest* and *kind*. A "good person" would be someone you'd like as a neighbor, as a politician representing you, as a teacher for your kids.

As you read those adjectives, you probably noticed that many of them—six of nine—link up nicely with the charitable impulse: *caring*, *compassionate*, *fair* (as in a desire for social justice), *generous*, *helpful* and *kind*.

In other words, *good people make gifts*.

Yet how many charities bother to celebrate such baseline values in their donor communications?

Very few I run across. And I review hundreds of items a year: direct mail appeals, donor newsletters, emails, websites, annual reports, videos, case statements, "thank-yous" and so on.

Instead, by and large, the donor communications I see say the wrong things. Almost none are donor centered. No wonder it's easy to make extraordinary gains in giving once you start talking differently.

United Way of Pickens County (SC) president and CEO Julie Capaldi embraced donor-centricity with unrestrained joy in her 2014–2015 Gratitude Report. Shown here: the cover and the opening spread.

Last word goes to Jeff Brooks, one of America's most experienced and successful direct mail copywriters, author in 2015 of *How to Turn Your Words Into Money:*

> Your donors are not *your* donors—as in, an asset you own or control.
>
> But your organization is *their* charity—something they use to accomplish their goals.
>
> Keep this distinction in mind, and your fundraising will be a lot better.

What every communication from your organization should (subliminally) say

No matter what words you actually choose, your prospects and your donors should hear something like this from you loud and clear, over and over and over and over and over:

> **Thank you.**
>
> **You make it possible.**
>
> **Thank you . . . SO, SO MUCH.**
>
> **This mission depends on you UTTERLY.**
>
> **And you know, here's a little secret I probably shouldn't reveal: at board and staff retreats, we always end up talking about YOU, the donor . . . the true believer, the supporter, the *real* family member.**
>
> **We talk about how important you are. Who keeps us strong and cutting edge?**
>
> **Donors like you.**
>
> **Philanthropists. Like you.**
>
> **We talk about YOU . . . and how all these special, compassionate, selfless people like you make SO MUCH possible.**
>
> **Frankly, we gush about you.**
>
> **I hope you don't mind.**
>
> **We gush about you shamelessly.**
>
> **Because you joined "the fight."**
>
> **You consulted your heart. You felt those crazy "caring" enzymes rise inside you.**

You glowed . . . like a high-wattage LED bulb of doing good.

You flared . . . into a nova star of doing good.

You screamed . . . with righteous purpose at the very moment you made your gift.

Or so we hope.

Because of people like you, we continue to hope.

Would it embarrass you to say the above?

Good. You *should* be embarrassed. That's when you know you've gone far enough.

Donors, however, won't be embarrassed. Applaud them without reservation. They'll love you for it.

By the way, if a board member or boss disagrees with this advice, that disagreement is clear proof of naïveté, ignorance or incompetence in the donor-relations arena. Now you know.

The cover and an inside page from a Community Legal Aid (Worcester, MA) annual report soaked in donor love.

Agents of Good "Principles of Donor Love"

Founded by John Lepp and Jen Love (she's second-generation; her dad is David Love, a legendary Canadian fundraiser), Agents of Good (AOG) is a Toronto-area fundraising agency devoted to donor-centricity.

Their elite client list includes cross-Canada brand name charities as well as fabulous local charities and a few lucky US nonprofits. These are the published, approved and followed AOG Principles of Donor Love:

Principle 1: You make your donor the hero. Every day. Every DM piece. Every email. Give them the opportunity to fix the world. They WANT to help. They WANT to fix something. They WANT to make an impact. Like Jen always says, it's that simple but critical shift from talking about "what we do" to "what you make possible."

Principle 2: Share amazing and inspiring stories. Every time your beloved donor hears from you, you want them to be re-engaged, re-energized and fall in love with you all over again. Your stories should provoke an emotional response in your donor.

Principle 3: Connect to your donors' values and emotions. Bottom line: money follows value. Think about your organization, think about that 24 hours before it existed. It was founded, likely, out of the desire by a few restless and innovative people to create change, to fix something. Your donors today hold those same values. It is through your shared values that your organization can give your donors a powerful sense of belonging.

Principle 4: Falling—and staying—in love. Good donor care is a courtship. A relationship. What metrics do you use to know when it is time for a second date? To go steady? Get engaged? Have you thought about your #donorlove story from the point of view of your donor? When are you surprising them? When are you asking for help? How are you getting to know *them* better?

Principle 5: Ask for one thing. Donors want to help fix something and feel really good about it. So, what's the problem and how can your donor be the solution? You need to make it easy and make it feel good! (In other words, scrap that coupon with the 28 check boxes and 7-point type, please!)

Principle 6: Who (or what) is the right voice for your story? You have the privilege and responsibility to speak on behalf of a community of like-minded citizens. It's also your job to echo what they feel passionate about and give them a chance to take action for what they believe. So, what, exactly, are you asking for AND who is the right voice for that question?

Finally, **Principle 7: Say thanks with passion.** Not "On behalf of . . . " Not "We received your cheque on . . . " Not "Yours sincerely . . . " Say thanks with passion! To borrow Tom Ahern's phrase, "pour love juice all over it!" Use emotion! Creativity! It's not the job of your executive director or the director of development—everyone should have a hand in gratitude. But whoever is doing it, whenever they may be doing it—please make sure they do it with real passion.

CHAPTER 10

Does your charity come across as an egotistical maniac?

First impressions count, as we all know.

An international child development charity asked me to evaluate its communications. So I went to the charity's home page, as a typical first-time visitor might. And what did I find there?

On the home page, this charity talked about itself 15 times in various featured items. On the other hand, it talked about the donor's role in the mission just once. And even that measly mention was in the context of the organization: "What are we doing and how can you help?"

A 15-to-1, WE-to-YOU ratio will not make you many new friends. It's resoundingly imbalanced and non-donor-focused. Unfortunately, it's an imbalance quite common in the nonprofit world.

What does *your* home page tell the world? Does it say loud and clear that donors are *vital*? Does it say loud and clear that donors are *welcome*? *Needed*? *Beloved*? *Desirable*?

It should, to maximize income. Just having a "donate" button will not do the job.

Most nonprofits seem deeply in love . . . with themselves, and it shows, in ways big and small. Here's one of the biggies.

The important distinction between *corporate* communications and *donor* communications

I'll be honest: it took me awhile to figure this distinction out.

I was poorly prepared professionally. I'd earned a credential in business communications, my ABC from the International Association of Business Communicators. I was trained to write about how great a company was, to make a publicly traded company look tantalizing to investors. I'd worked successfully in public relations. I knew how to pitch a story to the business press.

But there's the problem: donors *aren't* investors; not really, not technically, not in the traditional sense as understood on Wall Street. As Warren Buffett said, in his signature plain style: "Investing is laying out money now in order to get more money back in the future."

Are donors investors?

No, technically speaking.

Donors to charity reap no financial gain from laying out their hard-earned money. That's exactly what makes our work "non profit." Per Wikipedia: "A non-profit organization is an organization that uses its surplus revenues to further achieve its purpose or mission, rather than distributing its surplus income to the organization's shareholders as profit or dividends."

In the for-profit world, we talk about how fabulous our organization is in order to lure investors.

Investors want to make money. We show them why they will likely do so by placing their bet on our stock. We talk about our great products and services. We talk about our incredible rosy future, as we disrupt fading, legacy industries and gobble up market share from our fumbling competitors.

But that boasting approach is inappropriate in fundraising.

In fundraising, talking about how great your organization is actually *prevents* people from achieving a deeper emotional connection with you.

Let me sum this up, so we can move on:

- Corporate communications are about how great the *organization* is. It's the worst choice of voice for fundraising. It gathers only the lowest of low-hanging fruit.
- Donor communications are about how great the *donor* is. Switching to a donor-focused voice can multiply a charity's fundraising harvest 2, 3 . . . even 10 times.

Corporate comms are different than donor comms

Burn that distinction into your brain . . . and your nonprofit's communications will make more money.

Ignore that distinction . . . and your communications will always underperform.

Who's the hero?

The subject line of the email was perfect: "Tom, we really value your opinion." It came from the head of Oxfam Australia. I was excited and ready to share.

Then I opened it. "Hi Tom, Oxfam's work to change lives around the world only happens because of people like you . . . ."

What's wrong with that, you might wonder? After all, it gives me, the donor, plenty of credit.

True: but it gives the organization more credit first and puts me in a supporting role. The underlying message: *I'm not changing lives; Oxfam is.*

A simple rewrite would fix the problem:

"Hi Tom, Thanks to your generosity and that of others like you, lives around the world really are changing for the better."

This rewrite features the donor, not the organization. The donor, not Oxfam, is first and foremost.

"Nitpicking?" you reasonably wonder.

Trust me, minor details like this, piling up over time, matter. They (not your logo) become your brand in the donor's mind. They cumulatively produce more revenue and longer retention. And you'll never know how much they matter unless you change the way you talk.

Takeaway: Get out of the habit of talking about your organization as the hero. Start treating your donor as the hero instead.

CHAPTER 11

Raising awareness does not raise funds (usually)

"We need to raise awareness!" demands the board chair.

"If only we had more visibility in our community," laments the ED, "our fundraising problems would be over."

Chasing "increased visibility" is a well-meant remedy. Boards and bosses love the idea. It seems like such an obvious, reasonable and easy solution. "If our little charity were better known, we'd be rolling in dough."

Well, maybe that happens if you're a global celebrity like Mother Teresa. Or Oprah features you on her show. Or you're the beneficiary of some viral gimmick, as the ALS Association was in 2014 with the Ice Bucket Challenge. Or you're willing to spend $2 million for a Hollywood-quality ad and splash it over everything from TV to streetcar wraps, as the Hospital for Sick Children in Toronto did in 2016, to launch a $1.3 billion capital campaign.

But that's not really you, is it?

Let's say you get a little jolt of local visibility. Let's say a local newspaper . . . or an online local news service . . . or the local talk-radio personality notices your organization's work for one news cycle.

What happens next?

Maybe 2 people contact you. If the talk-show person included a strong call to action, maybe 10 people contact you. Maybe nobody contacts you. You know what? *Likely* nobody contacts you.

Chasing "awareness" is a waste of time, fundraising experts know

Up first: Jeff Brooks, from his blog, Future Fundraising Now:

"Some 'marketing experts' would have you believe fundraising is a two-step process: First you must make prospective donors 'aware' of your organization, then you can ask them to give."

We've heard from Jeff before, and why not? He's among America's most experienced and successful fundraisers.

"Two-step fundraising is a colossal waste of money. You basically double your cost and get nothing in return. The truth is, if you have limited resources, there's almost no way you can justify spending them on awareness campaigns. For the awareness campaign to be worthwhile, it would have to improve fundraising by 67%. If you've been in fundraising for more than a couple of years, you know how unlikely that is. The reality is that most awareness campaigns make *no measurable difference* for fundraising campaigns."

Up second: Tobin Aldrich, who, among other achievements, led World Wildlife Fund UK to new fundraising heights:

He wrote in his blog, "One of those counter-intuitive things about fundraising is that people don't actually have to have heard about your charity before [they'll] respond to a fundraising ask. I've lost count of the times I've been told by smart, senior people with a marketing background in some famous company that the first thing <insert name of non-profit here> must do is get our name out or raise awareness of the cause. Only then should we start asking for money. So let's start with a big awareness raising campaign (hey, maybe we could get an ad agency to do it for free!)

"Sorry but that's bollocks basically. The first thing any non-profit should do is fundraise. When you fundraise you tell people about your cause, you make them care about it and they give you money as a result. And do you know what, you raise money and awareness too. It's amazing, isn't it?"

Up last: Ireland's Ask Direct founder, Damian O'Broin. He ran a real-world test.

Results? If your charity spent £500,000 on competent direct mail fundraising, you brought in 4,000 gifts. If your charity put £200,000 into awareness with the other £300,000 put into direct mail fundraising, you brought in 3,000 gifts: 25% fewer. Why would anyone do that?

In sum: "Raising awareness" is a loser's priority.

"Raising awareness" is a passive, wait-and-see, hope-and-pray approach to fundraising. Non-specialists love it. Board members who hunger to be helpful love it. Board members who want to put off their fundraising duties as long as possible also love it (beware).

REAL fundraising is proactive: "Let's get to work, people! Get out there and ask!"

Set SMART goals instead

You've likely heard of SMART goals. The familiar acronym stands for specific, measurable, agreed upon, realistic, time-based.

SMART goals sound like this: "The goal of our fourth-quarter direct mail appeal will be to increase membership in our organization by 10 percent."

DUMB (daft, unrealistic, misunderstood, backwards) goals sound like this: "We need to raise community awareness. Money will follow."

There are exceptions . . . if you're good at PR

In 2017, Mike McKenna, community engagement coordinator at Wood River Land Trust in Idaho, wrote me to say: "I think you are seriously missing the boat with this advice—and we've got the checks to prove it!"

Mike was reporting on a media campaign he ran that raised "nearly a million dollars in less than a month."

Mike is a 15-year veteran journalist and editor. He knows angles. He knows stories. He knows what exactly sells to news outlets. Here's a bit of what Mike did:

> By creating strong relationships with local and regional media members in particular—and by trying to customize what we create for them so that it will interest their followers/fanbases—we've been able to increase awareness and then directly our financial support.
>
> For example, a simple recent press release sent to the right sources became newspapers stories that we can directly credit for raising nearly a million dollars in less than a month. All with no hard costs for advertising, just a little staff time to write and disseminate the information, which we also shared via social media and direct emails to our current donors—who did not supply as much money as the random people who walked in off the streets to donate.
>
> We also put on a free public event/concert this year that not only provided thousands in random donations once people realized who we are and what we do, but also gained us contact information from hundreds of potential donors, all while getting tons of touches and helping brand ourselves to thousands who attended or saw the ample media coverage.

Mike didn't specify what his land trust needed money for.

But it must have been a compelling project for people out of the blue to start making gifts near a million without a strong call to donate. The same kind of response filled the coffers when the 2010 Haiti earthquake, killing more than 100,000 people, hit world news. Hundreds of millions of dollars in donations poured in almost overnight, from all corners of the globe.

It won't happen for you: 99 percent guaranteed.

P.S. How to hire a journalist to assist fundraising

I've always thought the collapse of the print news industry worldwide had a silver lining, as a windfall for ambitious nonprofits.

When you hire a professional journalist, the hard part's already done: that person is already trained to write entertaining stories. That's what journalists do. They tell stories to help the facts go down.

"All" you, the nonprofit, have to do is explain how fundraising communications work . . . and hang a few more things on the new hire's tool belt like donor-centricity and sales copywriting techniques.

It probably doesn't hurt to have a whip-sharp hand at the beginning. There's a pretty big change these professionals will have to swallow.

You're not hiring them to be journalists anymore; make that absolutely clear in the interview. This will NOT be *yet another* job in their prior trade, a trade that did not have to produce revenue directly. This is about bringing in gifts, not storytelling for the sake of storytelling. Just saying.

CHAPTER 12

Why you actually matter to donors[1]

A case for support, in my opinion, is not very much about what your organization *does*: the daily activities, how it works, the operating hours, the staff, the names of programs, and a thousand other mundane details.

I believe a case is mostly about your *promise*, the promise you make to the world through your mission, your accomplishments, and your plans. Call it "the big picture."

A decade ago, Maureen Welch, then at the Antiquarian and Landmarks Society in Connecticut, sent a plea. She asked me to consider writing a book titled *Who are you kidding: Help for non-essential nonprofits.*

Her suggestion was a jest. But not entirely. There are plenty of nonprofits that suspect they're in a similar fix: nice but non-essential, and therefore not very compelling or competitive in the philanthropic marketplace.

Soon after she wrote, the Society changed its name to Connecticut Landmarks. It is a first-rate outfit. It manages, preserves, and opens to the public a distinguished portfolio of magnificent old homes dating as far back as 1678. They are lovely relics. Still, Maureen found it hard to imagine what case for support she could propose that would tug at donors' heartstrings like charities can that improve the world or ease suffering.

Maureen, this chapter's for you.

There's no such thing as a generic "donor"

Trust me, "non-essential" charities: you have your donors. You just have to find them. Will you find thousands? Perhaps not; not every charity has mass-market appeal. But there are certainly people out there who share your interests.

People seldom give to a charity by mistake. They're likely to give because a charity's mission has personal meaning for them. A short list:

1 This chapter first appeared in my book on case writing, *Seeing Through a Donor's Eyes*. The concepts mentioned are so important to your success that I felt it needed to be updated and included in this book as well.

- They want to give back. "I had no idea what to do with myself as kid. But college opened up a wide new world. It's been a good life since."
- They have special interests. "I love hiking these woods. It makes me feel twice as alive!"
- They have cherished priorities. "I saw my father die from that disease. I'm going to help until they find a cure."
- They have firm beliefs. "It's the art and the artists that make this city an exciting place to live."
- They have experiences and memories. "A mentor at the right time changed my life more than once. Everybody should be so lucky."
- They have values. "Every child deserves a shot at a good education."

Take me, for instance. Could Connecticut Landmarks land me as a donor?

It depends. One thing definitely works against them in my particular case: I don't live in Connecticut. And people do like to give locally where they can see (and even experience) the results themselves.

Still, like lots of people, I value history. I read history books for pleasure—and to gain perspective on current affairs.

To my history-loving eyes, therefore, the society's work is not that much about saving buildings from ruin. That *is* the fundamental activity, sure. But that's not why the society might matter to me.

And here we come to a nub.

You matter—but maybe not for the reason you think

You might think your mission is one thing while your donors feel it's something else.

Connecticut Landmarks describes its mission this way on its website: "[Our] mission is to inspire interest and encourage learning about the American past by preserving selected historic properties, collections and stories and presenting programs that meaningfully engage the public and our communities."

It also describes itself this way: "Founded in 1936 as the Antiquarian & Landmarks Society, we are a state-wide network of twelve significant historic properties that span four centuries of New England history. Our museums are starting points, 'landmarks in every sense,' for deeper exploration and greater appreciation of the Connecticut experience. We have something for everyone: from captivating house tours to lovely historic gardens, history celebrations and remarkable collections of art and antiques. Our real-life stories, as told through our collections, make history matter."

Not a bad nutshell, all in all.

But does it reflect a donor's interests?

You might want to write *two* mission statements. One, the in-house one, serves as a rudder for the board and staff. The second should be relevant to donors.

The donor-specific mission statement

Organizations are chronically unable to distinguish between activities and accomplishments. This leads to no end of trouble.

Connecticut Landmarks, for example, knows to the penny all the time and treasure that goes into maintaining its stellar collection of properties. So it assumes preservation is its primary mission. That's the insider's point of view.

But outsiders' (i.e., donors') points of view are different. They derive from an array of personal interests:

- I might be into house restoration myself, for instance, and be interested in construction techniques of a certain period.
- I might collect antiques and be interested in the milieu, when today's antiques were objects in everyday use.
- I might have an interest in local history because of my family origins.
- I might be a set designer interested in period interiors for a play.
- I might have an affectionate interest in a certain period in history that a particular house represents.

And so on. Buildings preserve more than bricks, boards, and furnishings; they preserve the ways of life lived in them, the tools employed to build them, the struggles of their eras: human history, in other words . . . and all the things that history does for us (entertain, inform, lend perspective, shock, surprise, remind).

Each building preserved by Connecticut Landmarks is a time machine. It can authentically take us to a different period. And without Connecticut Landmarks and its donors, these increasingly rare time portals won't survive. That's how slender is the thread on which authentic history hangs.

Historic buildings are endangered species; there are fewer of them left every year. Dr. Robert Cialdini, author of the *New York Times* business best seller, *Influence: The Psychology of Persuasion*, spotlights what he calls the "scarcity" principle. It's one of his "six most fundamental principles of influence."[2]

---

2 Dr. Cialdini's other principles of influence are discussed later in this book, in the chapter called "Triggers."

In fundraising it goes something like this: if you tell me something I value is in danger of disappearing, I will instinctively want to save it. An appeal that talks about what I stand to lose is even more powerful than an appeal that talks about what I stand to gain.

A donor mission statement for Connecticut Landmarks might then well begin, "Without Connecticut Landmarks and the donors who stand behind it, these one-of-a-kind historical treasures—and the lessons they continue to teach us about our world and theirs—will be lost forever."

Now that's an emotional pitch even an out-of-stater like myself can relate to.

An essential exercise for non-essential nonprofits: "What if we disappeared tonight?"

The following is an exercise I strongly recommend for *all* nonprofits, whether they suffer from "non-essential-itis" or not.

This dirt-simple but deeply revealing exercise forces you to zero in on why your organization and its activities really matter to outsiders. Guaranteed: the fresh perspectives you uncover will help you create fundraising communications that are far more persuasive.

Here's what you do.

Gather a half-dozen or more stakeholders in a room: staff; board; donors, too, if you can. Pose this problem: *Let's pretend. Let's pretend our organization and its programs disappeared tonight. Tomorrow, we're gone. What will the world/the community/individuals regret having lost?*

This is not a make-work exercise. This is a core exercise. Attendees in my workshops who try this exercise for even a few minutes are surprised, and then empowered, by what they discover about their organizations' true importance and impact.

In their business bestseller, *Made to Stick*, Chip and Dan Heath warn organizations against the "curse of knowledge": the creeping inability of insiders to see themselves the way outsiders (e.g., donors with all their many values, concerns, interests, and connections) do.

This curse can quickly make your nonprofit communications irrelevant to the donor: you (insider) talk about things that do not matter to the donor (outsider), in ways that do not persuade. Going through the exercise of asking—*If we were to disappear tonight, what would the world shed tears over losing?*—helps break the curse of knowledge and gives you well-grounded answers to that most important of questions: *Why would a donor care about the things we do?*

Wheels Down

CHAPTER 13

Do you have a "case for support"?

"Why should I give you my hard-earned money?"

The answer to that unabashed question is what's called your "case for support." Here's what others have to say on the same topic:

- In its simplest form, the case for support is a philanthropic investment prospectus: a straightforward document that tells prospective donors what your organization hopes to accomplish with their philanthropic gifts. (The Benefactor Group)
- Your case for support (sometimes called your "case statement") is one of the most important documents you can write for your non-profit. It forms the basis for all of your donor communications and "asks," and provides a valuable resource to everyone who is soliciting donations on your behalf. (Joe Garecht, The Fundraising Authority)
- A Case for Support is essentially the rationale for supporting you . . . it must answer any question anyone could possibly raise about your organization. (George Stanois, managing director of The Goldie Company; writing the case is Step 1 of George's "12 essential steps to fundraising success")
- The 'case for support' is the cornerstone of any fundraising activity. It captures who you are, what you do, what your goals are and why people should join with you to achieve these goals. It is informative and inspirational and is the touchstone for all the communications that support your fundraising. (CASE, the association for higher ed fundraisers)
- An organization's case for support is ultimately your message to your donors—why should they give to your organization? If this is all we ever thought about with a case for support, we'd be fine. (Andrew Brommel, Campbell & Company)

Andrew Brommel also offers some authoritative tips on writing, from his 2013 hour-long YouTube video, "Case Development 201":

1. **Have conviction. Make a strong statement.**

   Weak: Our university helps students build the skills they need to become leaders.

   Stronger: We believe every student has the power to lead.

2. **It's not about you. It's about the people you serve.**

   Weak: We believe our community needs a healthcare provider committed to caring for us all.

   Stronger: We believe everyone in our community deserves great healthcare.

3. **Think voiceover, not prose. Short and to the point.**

   Weak: Among all the ways we can invest in our school's future, the endowment is the most important, ultimately surpassing the impact of capital and program investments.

   Stronger: The endowment is the most important investment we can make in our school's future.

4. **Don't say everything. Say what matters.**

   Weak: As a nonprofit, community-based organization, we rely on the philanthropic support of our donors and neighbors to make our work possible.

   Stronger: Only you can make our work possible.

Tangible's Four Pillars Exercise

In 1993, Stephen Pidgeon set up Target Direct with two colleagues. That small start in someone's extra room grew into Tangible, a leading UK fundraising agency. Tangible has had nearly every "top 50" UK charity as a client at one time or another.

Along the way, Tangible developed, copyrighted and now generously shares with the world its Four Pillars Exercise.

Stephen describes the exercise in glorious depth, case studies and all, in *How to Love Your Donors (to Death)*. Let me give you an introduction, though. (You should still buy his book; it's worth the time and money.)

The Four Pillars Exercise exhausts . . . and reveals. (Both good.) The point of the exercise is to create a simple fundraising proposition that answers what Stephen calls his "killer question," namely: "Why should I give your charity £200 now?"

That's Stephen's personal "no questions asked" price point. He can donate £200 to what he sees as a worthy charity, without a second thought. That particular amount will not change his lifestyle, in other words. My personal charity price point these days is around US $150. If I can change a life for around $150, I will. An average donor in America might give $30–$50, if acquired without premiums.[1] Everyone's price point will be different; it depends on how rich you feel at the moment.

There are four pillars: Vision, Enemy, Hero, Recipient. I think Stephen got three out of those four dead right.

- "The **Vision** describes the charity's ultimate goal, the pinnacle of success that means the charity has no more work to do. . . ." This is your furthest stretch . . . way beyond today's realities. As Stephen notes, "It is the nature of this Vision that it will never be reached."
- The **Enemy** is simple—*what* evil, *what* misfortune or injustice, *right now*, prevents your Vision from being achieved.
- The third pillar is the **Hero**. "The Hero is a principle, a team, a person that is fighting the Enemy to achieve the Vision." Stephen specifically rules out the donor as hero. I disagree, with deep respect. I believe the Hero *is* the donor and is a critical part of the "team" Stephen refers to. When he quit Tangible, there was no good research to say that the donor might be best suited for the hero role in this classic story formula. But as it happens, I've conducted some of that very research for almost a decade (2008–2017) inside a major hospital system in southern California. I now know, for nonprofit community hospitals in the United States anyway, that positioning the *donor* as hero can yield FAR more revenue from the same contributor base: twice as much, three times as much, ten times as much. Simply put: "donor centricity," in my experience, produces significantly more charitable income. Many charities and creative agencies agree. The proof continues to roll in.
- The last pillar is the **Recipient**. "The Recipient is the person that benefits [from what your charity does]."

Stephen Pidgeon makes several essential points, in my perhaps distorted view:

1. when you weren't looking, your **vision** probably changed; one national cancer society stopped talking about "curing" cancer after a half-century of little progress on that front. It began instead talking about "defeating" cancer, as treatments improved and the lifespans of those the cancer-afflicted lengthened;
2. defeating an **enemy** is essential to rouse the troops;
3. "people give to people": hence stories about those **recipients** are crucially important; and
4. you will never lack donors if you make them **heroes**.

---

1 When premiums such as self-sticking return address labels are included in a direct mail pack, response rates rise but average gift amounts fall.

CHAPTER 14

How to figure out your case

I learned how to write a case from three masters:

1. Jerry Panas, author of (among other useful books) *Making a Case Your Donor Will Love: The Secret to Selling the Dream*. Jerry's the founding executive partner at Jerold Panas, Linzy & Partners (Chicago). He phoned me out of the blue one day in 2003. "I hear you can write. Can you fly to St. Louis this weekend?" Thus began my first-ever case.

2. Ron Arena, senior consultant and principal, leader of strategic communications at Marts & Lundy, the world's first fundraising consultancy, founded in the Unuted States in 1926. Ron recruited me in 2005 as a contract case writer. Over a good lunch that day, he shared with me his bare-bones analysis of what cases must contain. I still use his ideas in every case I write. His advice: "Just answer the three big questions." (See chapter 15.)

3. Busted projects. Maybe a third of the cases I worked on in the early years never reached the public for one reason or another. The project collapsed because of politics (that cancer center in Canada). The approval process was poorly strategized (ignore deans at your peril, college fundraisers). Somebody high up didn't like the writing (I never quite got the hang of Lutheran mysticism). Live and learn.

Breaking the Curse of Knowledge

I let my case clients know right away: "I'm your designated idiot."

By which I mean I'm looking at stuff as an outsider, not an insider, would.

Here's why being a designated idiot is in fact best practice.

As mentioned earlier, the 2007 business best-seller, *Made to Stick: Why Some Ideas Survive and Others Die*, by brothers Chip and Dan Heath, found that a chief reason for poor communications success was a phenomenon they dubbed "the Curse of Knowledge."

What's the nature of this awful curse?

Insiders (staff and board) simply know too much. And they like to talk about what they *know*. The operational details. How it all works. The clever programs. The data. At the same time, they neglect to cover what outsiders (i.e., your prospective donors) care about: why any of it matters.

"Nobody is interested in what you do," fundraising expert Stephen Pidgeon insists over and over. "They are only interested in what happens when that work is done."

I.e., your results matter, nothing else.

To write a persuasive case, therefore, you need to grow a new set of eyes: outsider eyes, *donor* eyes. You'll need to become a designated idiot, just like me.

How do you sell donors on supporting something they either haven't heard of or don't know the value of? The cover of this case for support makes a bold claim for an annual week-long contest that attracts thousands of students from across America and around the world. The opening spread ("If you are reading this, chances are . . .") broadly sorts casual readers into two groups: those who care about the future of kids, hence are more likely to give (which is pretty much everyone, given our biological imperatives); and those who don't care as much, hence are less likely to give. This sorting process helps focus your target audience . . . and subtly flatters them as well. The second spread quickly fills in a blank for people new to National History Day. It's an efficient, fast start to a case. Creative by Maggie Cohn and Andrea Hopkins.

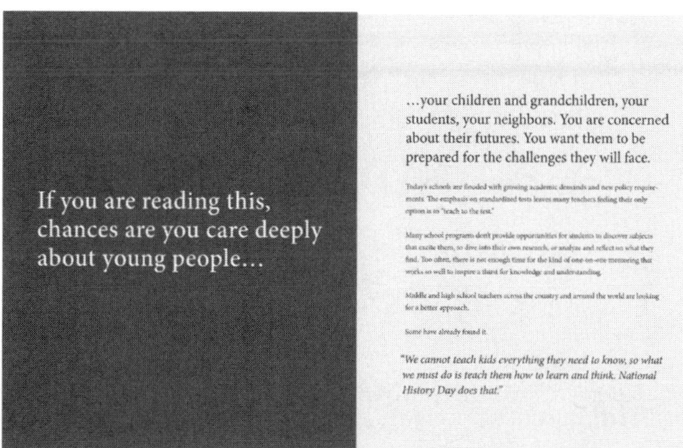

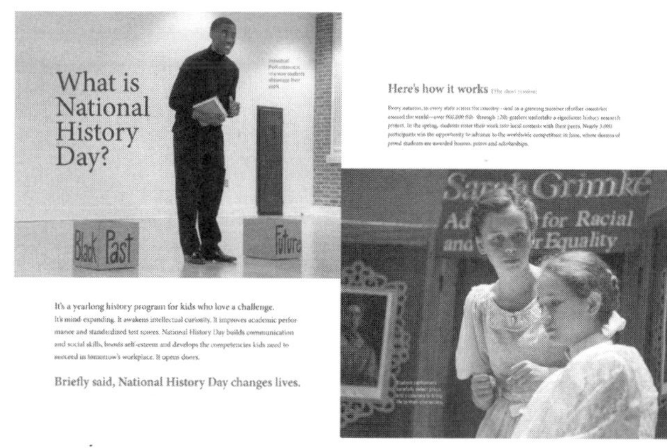

CHAPTER 15

"Make it bigger"

One of many things I learned from the celebrated Jerry Panas was this: "Make it bigger." As I understood the axiom, Jerry meant we should always make the case for support about *more* than the project or organization.

As he explains it,[1] the case isn't about building a new art museum. It isn't only about glass and steel and exhibits.

The museum's case is *also* about the busloads of kids who will arrive each year to learn about art and try their hand at it.

The museum's case is *also* about its gorgeous riverside site and how the new building will add excitement to the city's teensy bit dull River Walk.

Finally, the museum's case is *also* about bringing "thousands of families back into a fatigued downtown. It would be the centerpiece of a new cultural and arts area. It would reinvigorate and transform downtown. It would be an infusion of money and people for the downtown merchants."

---

1 Jerold Panas, *Making a Case Your Donors Will Love* (Medfield, MA: Emerson & Church, 2014): 31. [or "2014), p. 31."]

For years, faith ministries had sought state funding for affordable housing, to put a roof over the homeless. "It's the right thing to do!" they insisted. In response, there was abundant lip service, yet no serious funding ever resulted. A new advocacy coalition, HousingWorks RI, changed the message. The new message talked about sales clerks at Nordstrom's who couldn't afford an apartment near their work, so they slept in homeless shelters. The new message talked about teachers who couldn't find anything affordable in the communities where they taught. Same for police. Same for firefighters. Economic development is the one thing state legislators always care about. Three appropriations of $50 million apiece followed once the core message was changed. And it's all conveyed in the headlines; no need to read the small type to get the right message. Design by Orange Square Design.

CHAPTER 16

Ron Arena's Three big questions

I've written dozens of cases. All were built atop answers to the following three open-ended questions, in no particular order.

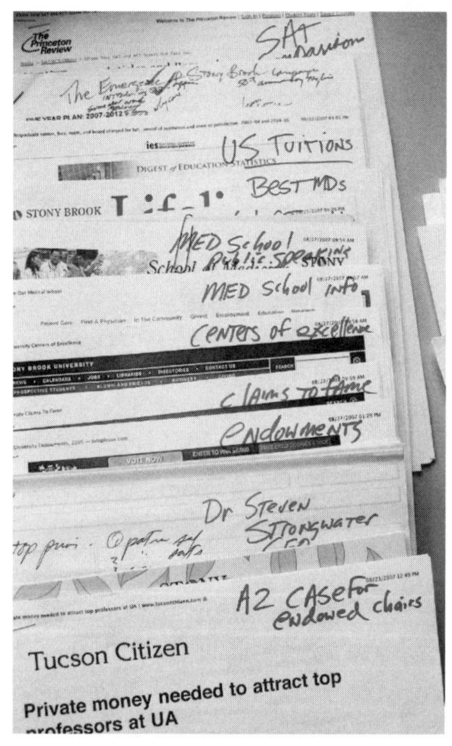

What my desk looks like as I prepare a case for endowed chairs at a university. What you're looking at is my "secondary research"; i.e., information downloaded from the Internet. Primary research comes from interviewing key informants.

Big Q #1. "Why us?"

This question should be easy enough: you're talking about how incredible your organization is. How impactful it is. How unique. How innovative. How well managed. How enduring ("Since the end of the First World War . . .").

If someone asked you at a party, "What does your nonprofit do?" the answer to "Why us?" might jump to tongue.

"We're a little, mission-driven place that wants to be recognized for providing the best care for the poorest people," as a med school president once said.

Or "We tell the full and fair story of the three-day battle where America's destiny was decided," as the Gettysburg Foundation might rightfully claim.

Or "Thanks to our long association with the Smithsonian, the Anchorage Museum is ideally equipped, scientifically and culturally, as well as by location, to tell the complex and rapidly changing story of the Arctic."

Or "Thanks to our best-in-class, fact-based sex education, the rate of unplanned pregnancies among suburban teens has fallen precipitously over the last two decades."

Or . . . whatever worthwhile thing your nonprofit does that no other organization is doing. In marketing parlance, it's known as your USP: Unique Selling Proposition. Agents of Good, a Toronto-based creative agency for fundraising, calls it your URG: the Unique Reason to Give.

Big Q #2. "Why now?"

What's the big hurry? Has something changed? Why is this appeal so urgent?

The right answer often is "If we don't do it now, bad things will continue to happen." Those won't be the exact words used, but that will be the message. I call it "selling the threat." With the right audience, it's irresistible.

The Yale Tomorrow capital campaign is a fine example of selling the threat.

Yale's case statement did a masterful job of cuing up the audience, with a single sentence floating alone on a white page: "Tomorrow, everything will be different." Ten pages of provocative predictions followed. My favorite: "Adults will be able to grow new teeth." (Amen to that.) The final prediction: "Two Asian universities will rank among the top ten in the world."

Yale has ranked on that same top 10 list so long you might think it's hereditary. Of course, it's not: elite universities compete globally and no holds barred for the best faculty and students. Maintaining a school's top-shelf status is very, very expensive.

The message from then-president Richard C. Levin gets quickly to the threat and returns to that theme over and over:

> I invite you to participate in Yale Tomorrow, a five-year, $3 billion campaign to build the future of our University. *I seek your support to ensure that the accomplishment of recent years is not remembered merely as a bright moment in Yale's long history*, [emphasis added] but rather as the foundation for a Yale of permanently greater breadth and strength, a Yale with the capacity to contribute—by means of its scholarship and its graduates—not only to the nation but also to the world.

> . . . the work of building and sustaining a great institution is never done. To expand Yale beyond its current scale and scope, to build the Yale of tomorrow, we will need new financial resources.
>
> To remain among the world's great universities, we must invest in science and technology on an unprecedented scale.
>
> Excellence is no excuse for complacency.

How did it do?

The Yale Tomorrow campaign ran from September 2006 to June 30, 2011, T-boned by the Great Recession. It raised in total $3.881 billion, well past its original goal of $3 billion. "More than 110,000 alumni, parents, friends, corporations, and foundations contributed to the Campaign, directing their gifts to every area of the University," purrs the press release.

But selling the threat by itself isn't enough. As a case for support, Yale Tomorrow would have been nothing without its comprehensive, far-reaching vision. The threat was there, but merely as a launching pad for a huge leap forward.

Yale Tomorrow is a staunchly "A-to-B" case.

Today, your organization is at point A. It's capable of just so much. Tomorrow, though, you want to be at some wonderful, new point B. *That's* your destination. Virtually every capital campaign I work on is an A-to-B case.

Urgency works

Urgency helps you overcome inertia. Inertia is a huge barrier in fundraising: let's face it, it's so much easier to do *nothing* than *something*.

That's why you make matching-gift appeals time-limited. The looming presence of a deadline ("To double your gift, we must receive it by December 31!") gets people off the sofa.

Urgency can also help a new campaign jump the queue.

If *your* problem is more urgent than somebody's else problem, maybe I'll give to you instead of them. Trends have built-in urgency and relevance. Global warming is a trend. Rising cancer rates are a trend. Economic injustice is a trend.

If you have a good trend, ride it.

Big Q #3. "Why you, the potential donor, might care?"

Answers to the first two questions—why is our organization uniquely qualified and why is this urgent—are fairly objective, once you've done your homework.

But the third big question is tricky. It's also where the fun begins, in this copywriter's opinion.

The truth is, we never know *entirely* why any individual gives. It might be simply "You asked. I gave." Or it might be a complex of hidden, interior, psychological reasons leading to the giving decision.

Some reasons are predictable; most causes have a "natural constituency." (Explained in the next chapter.)

Some reasons are at least guessable, thanks to decades of scientific research about human behavior.

But some reasons you'll never know for sure, because they're deeply private or subconscious.

The answer to the "Why you would care?" question is so delightfully complex it deserves its own chapter.

Let's wade in.

CHAPTER 17

In the mind of a donor

I don't recall exactly what year it was; maybe five years back?

British fundraiser Richard Radcliffe had by then already interviewed more than 17,000 donors[1] about one thing: why they gave.

And he said this to me that night, in the vicinity of a bar in the Netherlands: "Donors are staggeringly ignorant of the causes they support."

Lest ye misunderstand: Richard did not mean that was a bad thing, "staggering ignorance."

He meant, *Lucky us!*

He meant, *Lucky us! We don't have to explain very much to get a gift. People are already 99% of the way there, in their own minds. All we have to do is connect.*

Donors may well be ignorant of how your charity's evidence-based seven-point approach to poverty amelioration yields 13% better results amongst an at-risk urban youth population ages 15–25.

But!

What donors DO have in abundance are their own personal values, interests, beliefs, experiences, upbringing, lost loves, secret passions, regrets, fears, angers, hopes, and built-in empathy. Only psychopaths are immune to your wiles. They're born without the ability to feel another's pain. Most of us, though, are susceptible.

How to connect

Our most likely "first-time donor" prospects are already predisposed to give (for their own reasons). All they need is a proper ask.

Let's do a mental exercise. I'm going to try to sell you a car the way many nonprofits try to sell giving.

You: "I need a car."

Me: "Well, I have just the thing. It has four wheels."

You: "Hope so."

Me: "Plus, and this is cool: it has an engine."

---

1 By 2017, Richard's count was up to 25,000+ interviewed.

"OK."

"Oh, and you'll like this. You know how you can't see outside without windows. This car has windows."

"Un-huh."

"And, and, and . . . this gets me so excited . . . it has this device for sending the car in different directions. We call it a steering wheel."

"Is there anyone else around I can talk to?"

"No, wait. There's so much more. You don't even have to stand. Our car has seats!"

Charities love their programs—every bloody detail. But that's the Curse of Knowledge, as described in *Made to Stick*.

The assumption seems to be that if a charity blueprints all a program's details THEN the prospective donor will fall as deeply in love as the staff did. A stranger will then make a gift because, come on, who in their right mind *wouldn't* support this charity, knowing how great these programs are?

Sorry: that kind of thinking is for chumps . . . not champs.

It's no coincidence that Richard Radcliffe and Stephen Pidgeon both agree that a charity's program details are a waste of time in fundraising.

It's not because they're both Brits. It's because they're both experienced fundraisers with a professional's understanding of how to sell well. They know the difference between features and benefits. They know that features "tell" and benefits "sell." They know that the details of your programs, the statistics and technical complexities that insiders could talk about endlessly, are in fact your weakest hand.

CHAPTER 18

Natural constituencies

Every charity has its "natural constituency," people who are far more predisposed to look favorably on your appeal.

- A university has its proud graduates.
- Public radio has its avid listeners.
- A nonprofit hospital has its "grateful" patients (i.e., those NOT suing). Same for a visiting nurse association.
- Arts museums and theaters have those who would define themselves as "arts lovers."
- Faith-based charities have their believers and followers.
- Children have adults.
- Animal welfare charities like Lollypop Farm (Rochester, NY) and Soi Dog (Bangkok, Thailand) have animal lovers.
- Audubon and The Nature Conservancy and regional nature conservancies such as Ontario Nature have bird watchers (a vast hobby group) and self-described "nature lovers."
- Community foundations have the civic minded (and where bequests are concerned, people without heirs who are looking for a responsible place to leave their assets).

Like you, I breathe air and drink water to stay alive. That fact automatically makes me **predisposed** to care when I hear about an air or water quality problem. If your mission is to solve my air or water problem, then I am predisposed to support you. Every charity I can think of has *some* "natural constituency," i.e.:

- a group of people who are inclined by their own values, interests, experiences, upbringing (and such) to lean in your charity's direction.

Your natural constituency consists of those *most likely* to give your charity a gift.

The average person who has no personal connection is *least likely* to give.

Your natural constituency is the pool of prospects you turn to first with your appeal. "Everyone" is not a target audience.

Finding your natural constituents

The hard part, of course, is finding these well-qualified, most-likely-to-give households.

Talk about needles in a haystack.

And *this* book is about writing . . . not about hunting for donor prospects. But I will say this: first the Internet and search engines, and now the advent of social media, have made it far easier for causes and their natural constituencies to find each other.

In 2015, for instance, Soi Dog Foundation, a small animal welfare charity in Bangkok, Thailand, brought in more than $300,000 a month in gifts, about a third of that from American females 45 and older . . . mainly through Facebook.

That robust income stream, sourced from animal lovers worldwide, has allowed Soi Dog to expand its mission beyond rescue of homeless, neglected and abused street dogs ("soi" means "street" in Thai). Soi Dog is now making a serious dent in a national problem: Thailand's illegal and inhumane dog meat trade. Consider this factoid: it's widely believed among purchasers that skinning kidnapped dogs alive helps tenderize their meat.

You can imagine how readily animal lovers chip in to help with that cruel fight.

CHAPTER 19

Get them into a fight

The campaign for the 2008 US presidency saw a new fundraising phenomenon. For the first time in history, a candidate raised tens of millions, in contributions ranging from $100 to $250, from average American households. Never before had normal folk forked over this kind of dough. As you might suspect, the Internet helped enable this flood of populist cash.

But the Internet was not the cause.

Yale economics professor Dean Karlan studied the motivations behind these unprecedented political contributions. He quickly dismissed the "quid pro quo" angle. A *million*-dollar contributor might expect access, influence, and a night in Lincoln's bedroom. Not so, a small contributor.

"Giving is not about a calculation of what you are buying," Professor Karlan concluded (*New York Times*, March 9, 2008). "It is about participating in a fight." A fight you care about. A fight you feel could be won.

These millions of small contributors were angry with what they saw as a failed Republican administration. And they hoped Barack Obama's slogan of "Change we can believe in" was more than just words. So millions chose, with their gifts of $100 and $250, to get into a fight they felt was both winnable and worth the cost.

Emotional triggers rule

Anger and hope: two of the most powerful emotional triggers in your persuasion arsenal.

And it's never been easier to keep people in a fight, thanks to social media and email.

Keep the news from your front lines hot and fresh.

Keep it donor-centered.

Give people things to do other than simply making gifts. Have them call a politician's office and register their opinion. Have them sign a petition. Have them share a post: "Sharing is caring."

And acclaim every victory, no matter how minor (or odd) it may seem. Winning a big battle takes years. You'll need to sustain interest, momentum, and a sense that progress is being made, despite occasional setbacks.

Some good advice from Hal Malchow, veteran of dozens of political fundraising campaigns: "You'll raise far more money with news of a setback that leaves you in desperate need and your mission yet to be accomplished."

Don't get me wrong. You *should* celebrate your triumphs. But always leave room for accomplishing more, if only you had more resources. Your gains as an organization don't wipe out all the mission's needs. Give your true believers plenty of opportunities to renew their faith in you, by investing again. Show them your need. Give them plenty of chances to feel good because they helped meet the need.

And I'll reinforce that with one piece of anecdotal evidence.

We were writing newsletters for a Boys & Girls Club. When our front-page headlines emphasized triumph but neglected to mention need, giving in response to that issue fell. When our next issue came out, our front page emphasized triumph—yet also boldly stated, "But we can do more, if we have your help." Gifts in response jumped back to earlier, higher levels.

What's *your* fight?

You've heard it a thousand times: "Join the fight against cancer, heart disease, to end [fill in the blank], to restore [fill in the blank]."

"Getting people into a fight" is a very useful metaphor.

- It attracts like-minded people.
- It gets them pointed in the same direction, toward some desirable goal.
- It promises drama and conflict and reversals along the way (all good for storytelling . . . and fundraising).
- And it implies a fair chance of ultimate victory, with an evil defeated . . . the best story ending in the world!

Does all this sound suspiciously similar to "conducting a campaign"?

Bravo: you've a discerning mind.

Campaigning and "getting people into a fight" are one and the same.

Be prepared: insiders won't necessarily understand nor appreciate any metaphors about fighting, battles, or winning wars. I run into this a lot. Nonprofit staff and volunteers prefer nonviolent language on principle. Not on any *marketing* principle, you understand; simply because they're against violence in any form.

It's a perfectly understandable point of view. Aren't we all trying to make the world a better place? Haven't wars done enough damage, without dragging that kind of language into the nonprofit sector?

Don't be blinded by this insider timidity. It's a classic example of over-thinking. A good fight attracts committed supporters. A good fight is deeply emotional. A good fight well waged will satisfy your customers (i.e., your donors).

Michael's Story:
Arrest Record Destroys Plans to Serve His Country & Go to College, Despite Case Being Dismissed

At fourteen, Michael got in a fight with his stepbrother. His mother and his sister couldn't break it up so they called the police.

Michael was arrested and charged with assault. After meeting him and hearing what happened, the judge dismissed the case.

Four years later, Michael graduated high school and applied to the National Guard. His father had been in the military and Michael was eager to follow in his footsteps. This was also the only way he could afford to go to college.

The Guard rejected Michael's application because he had a record.

He'd thought the slate was clean once the charges were dropped. But, the damage had already been done.

Like many kids, Michael is left with a record that will haunt him well into the future...

It doesn't have to be like this. You can help.

☑ Yes! I believe in high school diplomas, not handcuffs. Let's keep kids in class and out of the courts.

I can help with a donation of:

☐ $250 ☐ $100 ☐ $50 ☐ $25 ☐ $______

☐ My check is enclosed. ☐ Please charge my card. (See reverse)

Name: ______

Address: ______

City: ______ State: ______ Zip: ______

Email: ______ Phone: ______

CfJJ Citizens for Juvenile Justice
44 School Street, Suite 400
Boston, Massachusetts 02108
www.cfjj.org 617-338-1050

Get me into a fight. This insert from a direct mail appeal tells the story of Michael, unfairly haunted by a juvenile criminal record the judge dismissed. The reply device reinforces the outrage. Written by Tina Cincotti, with design by Wendy Brovold.

CHAPTER 20

Focus on your target audience

I say this a lot in my workshops:

> You build success *backwards* from your target audience.

But what does the mantra actually mean?

Simply this: every gift you chalk up as a fundraiser will happen thanks to someone's brain making a decision to act.

Sometimes you can influence that brain's decision. But you do not *make* the decision for them. So . . .

What's on *their* minds? What is your *target audience* interested in? What do they think about? Wonder about? Care about?

The more you understand *me, the donor*—my whims, my fears, my desires, my angers, my background, my experiences, my self-image, my regrets—the more likely you are to make a sale.

Success in fundraising doesn't start with you. Success starts with your supporters . . . and who they are.

You build success backwards from your target audience.

A good way to spend your next staff retreat

Studying how the human mind works, and why it can occasionally be persuaded to rise from its habitual indifference and inertia, is what successful marketers obsess over, fundraisers in particular.

But can we face one bloody truth about our industry?

Fundraisers work at a massive disadvantage in today's highly engineered consumer economy.

Aside from a few tote bags, DVDs and naming opportunities, we don't typically exchange much of anything for the cash we need to sustain our missions.

We rely on the kindness of strangers; which, to our discredit, we poorly understand. Logically, in a perfectly selfish world, charity shouldn't even exist. Survival of the fittest, remember?

And yet charity, helping others, is a *massive* industry on every continent except Antarctica (for the obvious, uninhabitable reason).

It's not logical. It's just true.

Case study: Targeting the business community

It's the same whether you're selling appliances, veggie burgers . . . or your vision: *offering the right thing to the right people at the right time* makes the sale.

Repeatedly, relentlessly ask yourself: *What does our particular target audience care about? What does our particular target audience need? What promise might stir our particular target audience?*

Bow Valley College in Calgary hoped to offer a quality career education to twice as many students, so it embarked on a capital campaign to fund a campus expansion. Bow Valley is what's called a "community college" in the United States: it turns out graduates with precise skills.

Bow Valley identified a very particular target audience: local business leaders. Why them? Because businesses thrive when they have great employees. And that's exactly what Bow Valley turns out: job-ready graduates.

The Bow Valley student might enter as a single mom age 25 just looking for a way to feed her family . . . or a disillusioned college drop-out hoping to reclaim a future . . . or a recent immigrant with language deficiencies . . . or a university graduate with no marketable skills.

But the Bow Valley *graduate* is a reliable product: someone well trained, who knows a specific job inside and out, who knows how to behave properly in a Canadian office place, who won't need to be fired nine months down the road at great expense to the company.

Particular target audience meet *appropriate promise*: "We'll put twice as many of these wonderful employee candidates into the local pool, if you'll help Bow Valley College double in size."

Again: you build success backwards from your target audience.

EVERYBODY TALKS ABOUT JOB CREATORS. BUT WHAT ABOUT THE EMPLOYEE CREATORS?

Community colleges play an often-unappreciated role in a fast-paced, quick-change, leading-edge economy like Calgary's. After all, what do you do if your community has jobs but can't find qualified people to fill them? That's the special economic niche the best community colleges fill.

They graduate the practical nurses our hospitals desperately need. They graduate the qualified-from-the-get-go legal assistants our law firms crave. They graduate the administrative professionals who keep our offices running smoothly. And that's just a fraction of what they do.

Calgary is fortunate. In Bow Valley College, our community has one of Canada's finest, fastest, most innovative employee creators.

And, we create the lifelong learning opportunities that unleash the vast potential in every student, to launch and further a career, and contribute to our economy and our community.

With your farsighted help, an expanded Bow Valley College will be a mainstay of Alberta's expansive economic future.

Our Quest for BEST plan is ready to go. It just requires $20 million in investment from visionary individuals, corporations, and foundations.

Government is already at the table. Thanks to $271 million in government support, Bow Valley College has two outstanding new buildings in the heart of downtown Calgary. Come for a tour—you'll be impressed.

So, may we count you in for the Quest for BEST?

OUR HISTORY

1998/99
First Strategic Plan is created and is focused on Growth Through Partnerships.
NEW PROGRAM: Corporate Readiness Training Program (CRTP). International Recruitment and Marketing Officer is appointed to pursue growth opportunities.

1999/2000
New technology is harnessed to create a virtual student lounge with e-learning resources.
NEW PROGRAM: Life Skills Coach. Brokerage agreement with Lethbridge Community College for delivery of the Practical Nurse program. Partners with China, Zimbabwe, Guyana, and Hawaii for ESL instruction.

2000/01
34% of revenues are generated through entrepreneurial activities. Crowding in existing facilities sparks study of space requirements; determines that major expansion would be required in three to five years.

2001/02
Enrolment rises 15.5% with 40% enrolment increase in Health and Community Care programs. Centre is launched for Career Advancement and the opening of Career Connections.
NEW PROGRAMS: Accounting and Financial Management; Aboriginal Practical Nurse.

Bow Valley College's capital campaign aimed to pretty much double enrollment and campus size. The target audience was narrow: business leaders in the Calgary area capable of making major gifts. The case for support, therefore, devoted one spread to a problem that especially worries business leaders: the high cost of hiring the wrong people. Design: Bow Valley College.

CHAPTER 21

Donor communications 101

Communicating with donors consists of just three basic activities:

- You *ask* for my help.
- You *thank* me for giving you my help.
- Then you *report back* to me what kinds of good things happened, due to my help and the help of others. "Did giving matter? What did philanthropy achieve?"

Then you do it over and over and over. You never stop, per the good advice of Jim Shapiro and Steven Screen, The Better Fundraising Company. Their drumbeat: "Ask, thank, report, repeat."

And yet many charities have a big problem executing this simple routine well.

Asking does not operate in isolation

Asking is part of a system that brings in new donors and then tries desperately to cling to them, retaining very few on the whole.

Your most costly failures—low average gifts, poor retention of new donors, unrealized opportunities such as major gifts and bequests—will likely to be due to things as prosaic as your charity's limp thanks and lackluster reporting.

On the flip side: lively thanks and donor-centered reporting will yield your most lucrative successes. Those who are best at thanking are beloved back. And donor newsletters that say all the right things and deliver emotional gratification on a regular basis will always be welcome.

The monthly donor newsletter published by Nashville Rescue Mission, in the skilled editorial hands of Michelle Brinson, raises on its own more than $2 million in gifts annually, about a fifth of the total raised each year. For every dollar the Mission spends on overhead, production and mailing, the newsletter inspires almost $7 in additional giving.

This masterful front-page design is strong, consistent and focused. It includes a great close-up of a real person served by the mission; an honest smile to show things are getting better and a headline that always acknowledges the donor as the true savior. Emotional gratification is efficiently delivered in the first few seconds of the reader's encounter with the cover. Donors appreciate messages that flatter them; that's science.

Is Nashville's return on investment a fluke? Well, it's unusually high, true. But it's far from a fluke. Nashville is just another example of a competent donor newsletter built with the Domain Formula in mind.

Testing by Seattle's Domain Group in the 1990s proved that a nonprofit could **make just as much money from a newsletter sent to current donors as it could from its conventional appeals**, assuming your nonprofit followed the rules they established. Here's what they discovered:

- Competent printed newsletters sent to current donors raise $3.33 for every dollar spent on printing, postage and other costs.
- Competent direct mail appeals sent to current donors raise $3.22 for every dollar spent.

The ROI looks virtually the same; newsletters make 10¢ more per dollar spent. But there is a difference, a vast difference emotionally: appeals are often seen as a nuisance, newsletters are often seen as a reward.

Your Membership In Action: 2013

Ontario Nature members like you helped us achieve victories for nature right across our province last year. Here are just a few of the ways your membership was in action saving species you love and protecting spaces you explore.

Gutting the Endangered Species Act? No Way!
Our government gutted the legislation that protects endangered species. So we announced we were suing them. Together with our members, we have fought long and hard for important laws that protect nature, like our gold standard Endangered Species Act. Changing the rules means that projects like roads and quarries are protected while birds and turtles are not. Thank you for standing with us!

Reptiles, Amphibians and iPhones...Oh My!
Your support helped us develop and launch apps for iPhone and Android devices, allowing "citizen scientists" and volunteers to take photos of reptiles and amphibians, enter habitat information and submit their records to us instantly. Almost 1,000 new volunteers joined, adding 45,000 new records to our Reptile and Amphibian Atlas.

You Invested in Tomorrow's Environmental Leaders
With your support, we welcomed over 100 energetic young people from 49 different communities across Ontario to our Youth Summit for Biodiversity and Green Solutions. We were delighted to connect with 25% more teens than the year before!

The beautiful thing about the summit was that it gave me the connections and resources I would need to continue making a difference within my hometown. I was able to meet and create memories with incredible youth from all over Ontario, who, like myself, are all trying to change the world. – Noa, 16

Forest and Freshwater Foods
We collaborated with First Nations groups and other organizations to encourage our leaders to protect forest and freshwater food systems in Northern Ontario. Specifically, we were working to protect the land and waters that are the source of these foods, and nurturing local economies based on their sustainable harvest. Our work in 2013 culminated in the government amending the draft Local Food Act to include forest and freshwater foods. An important victory!

Thank you! Please turn over to see why your renewed support in 2014 is crucial!

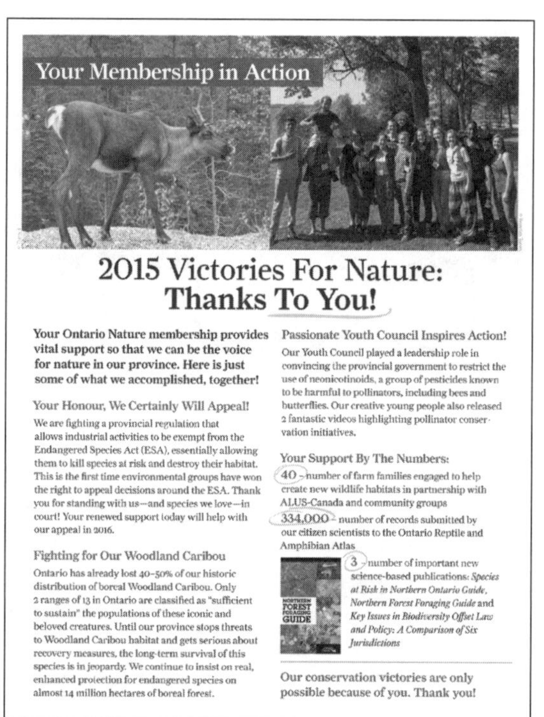

Your Membership in Action

2015 Victories For Nature: Thanks To You!

Your Ontario Nature membership provides vital support so that we can be the voice for nature in our province. Here is just some of what we accomplished, together!

Your Honour, We Certainly Will Appeal!
We are fighting a provincial regulation that allows industrial activities to be exempt from the Endangered Species Act (ESA), essentially allowing them to kill species at risk and destroy their habitat. This is the first time environmental groups have won the right to appeal decisions around the ESA. Thank you for standing with us—and species we love—in court! Your renewed support today will help with our appeal in 2016.

Fighting for Our Woodland Caribou
Ontario has already lost 40–50% of our historic distribution of boreal Woodland Caribou. Only 2 ranges of 13 in Ontario are classified as "sufficient to sustain" the populations of these iconic and beloved creatures. Until our province stops threats to Woodland Caribou habitat and gets serious about recovery measures, the long-term survival of this species is in jeopardy. We continue to insist on real, enhanced protection for endangered species on almost 14 million hectares of boreal forest.

Passionate Youth Council Inspires Action!
Our Youth Council played a leadership role in convincing the provincial government to restrict the use of neonicotinoids, a group of pesticides known to be harmful to pollinators, including bees and butterflies. Our creative young people also released 2 fantastic videos highlighting pollinator conservation initiatives.

Your Support By The Numbers:
40 – number of farm families engaged to help create new wildlife habitats in partnership with ALUS-Canada and community groups
334,000 – number of records submitted by our citizen scientists to the Ontario Reptile and Amphibian Atlas
3 – number of important new science-based publications: *Species at Risk in Northern Ontario Guide*, *Northern Forest Foraging Guide* and *Key Issues in Biodiversity Offset Law and Policy: A Comparison of Six Jurisdictions*

Our conservation victories are only possible because of you. Thank you!

Ontario Nature takes pains in its annual reports to thank donors and give them credit for the victories. But it also gives donors a clear responsibility, using headline statements such as "Your renewed support in 2016 is crucial." Creative by Agents of Good.

"Stop staring at my wallet. It makes me uncomfortable."

Charities tend to focus on what they worry most about: *How much money can be raised?*

So they are strongest in asking.

Where they are weaker is in thanking. Nonprofit thanks are often perfunctory, predictable, leaden and unconvincing; robotic, if electronically derived: "On behalf of [fill in the blank], the board and I wish to thank you for your generous gift today of [fill in the blank]." Result? A thousand "different" thank-yous saying pretty much the same thing.

Donors give to multiple causes. An average donor will see 10–20 thank-yous a year and promptly forget them all. You want to be the thanks they can't forget.

Finally, there's reporting.

Charities I review are *weakest* in their reporting—which is often simply clueless and emotionally dead, serving up stuff that only insiders care about, like a letter from the board chair breaking down the program stats.

There's a reason Heart of the Mission has a 7:1 return on investment. It delivers a real dose of special feeling about real people in every issue. As Harold Sumption, "the man who helped put Oxfam, Help the Aged and ActionAid on the map,"[1] insisted throughout his unrivaled career: "People give to people, not to organisations, mission statements or strategies."

Flattery gets you places

As Roger Dooley writes in *Brainfluence* (John Wiley & Sons, 2012), his book about using the findings of neuroscience in sales and persuasion, "Mom was wrong."

She preached that "flattery will get you nowhere." In fact, though, "research shows that even when people perceive that flattery is insincere, that [same] flattery can still leave a lasting and positive impression of the flatterer."

All flattery feels good, in other words. Your perfect mantra now becomes:

- Ask (and flatter)
- Thank (and flatter)
- Report (and flatter)

1 "Harold Sumption," *Independent*, April 21, 1998.

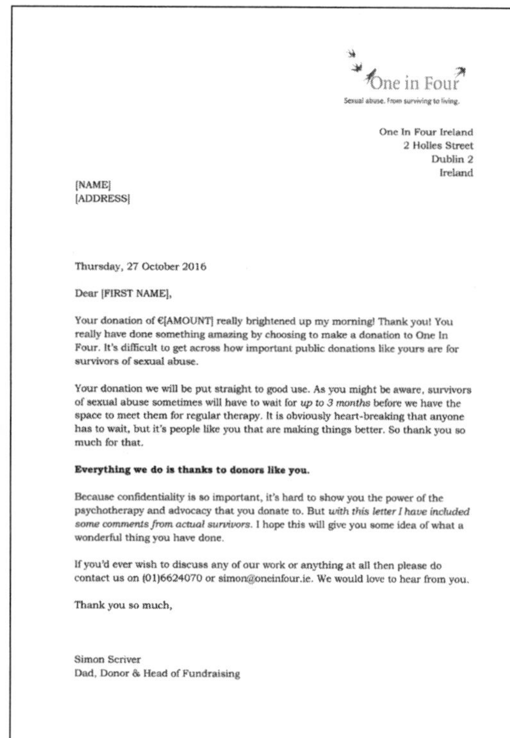

One in Four

Sexual abuse. From surviving to living.

One In Four Ireland
2 Holles Street
Dublin 2
Ireland

[NAME]
[ADDRESS]

Thursday, 27 October 2016

Dear [FIRST NAME],

Your donation of €[AMOUNT] really brightened up my morning! Thank you! You really have done something amazing by choosing to make a donation to One In Four. It's difficult to get across how important public donations like yours are for survivors of sexual abuse.

Your donation we will be put straight to good use. As you might be aware, survivors of sexual abuse sometimes will have to wait for *up to 3 months* before we have the space to meet them for regular therapy. It is obviously heart-breaking that anyone has to wait, but it's people like you that are making things better. So thank you so much for that.

Everything we do is thanks to donors like you.

Because confidentiality is so important, it's hard to show you the power of the psychotherapy and advocacy that you donate to. But *with this letter I have included some comments from actual survivors*. I hope this will give you some idea of what a wonderful thing you have done.

If you'd ever wish to discuss any of our work or anything at all then please do contact us on (01)6624070 or simon@oneinfour.ie. We would love to hear from you.

Thank you so much,

Simon Scriver
Dad, Donor & Head of Fundraising

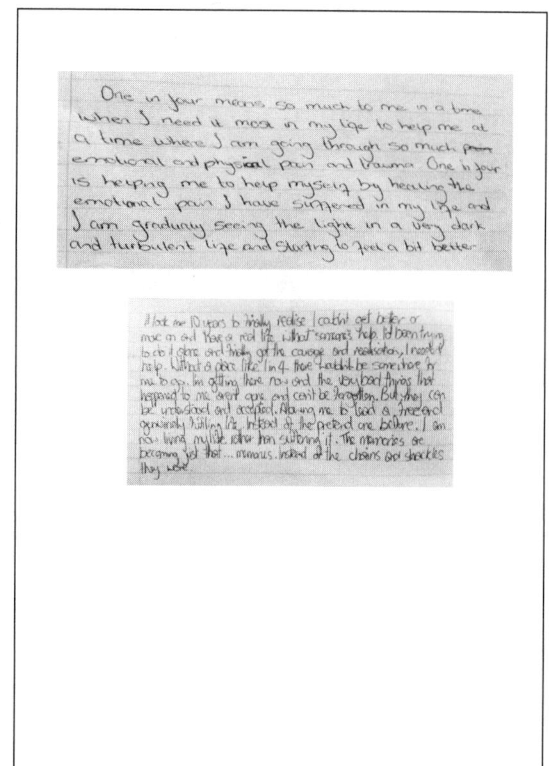

One in four means so much to me in a time when I need it most in my life to help me at a time where I am going through so much emotional and physical pain and trauma. One in four is helping me to help myself by healing the emotional pain I have suffered in my life and I am gradually seeing the light in a very dark and turbulent life and starting to feel a bit better.

It took me 10 years to finally realise I couldn't get better or move on and have a real life without someone's help. I'd been trying to do it alone and finally got the courage and realisation, I needed help. Without a place like 1 in 4 there wouldn't be somewhere for me to go. I'm getting there now and the very bad things that happened to me aren't gone and can't be forgotten. But they can be understood and accepted. Allowing me to lead a free and genuinely fulfilling life. Instead of the pretend one before. I am now living my life rather than suffering it. The memories are becoming just that... memories. Instead of the chains and shackles they were.

Simone Scriver at One in Four, Ireland, crafted this warm, emotional thank-you for first-time donors. It includes reproductions of actual testimonials from sexual abuse victims who were helped by the agency.

And don't be shy about it! Tell your donor often, loud and clear, in the big type, just how great she is. (And if you don't really believe that donors are all that great, well . . . I guess feel free to fake it. But ask yourself if you're in the right job.)

CHAPTER 22

How quickly should you thank a new donor?

In 2011, Damian O'Broin, founder and manager of Ask Direct in Ireland, made a presentation at the global IFC (International Fundraising Conference) in the Netherlands. He shared some startling research from McConkey Johnston International UK (now the Christian Fundraising Consultancy).

The research found that first-time donors who received a personal thank-you within 48 hours were four times more likely to give again. Yes: thanking in 48 hours = 400% improvement in renewal rates.

First-time donors are ardent. But that ardor cools fast if you don't sustain it.

It's like a campfire ignited by a match from tinder. You nurse it. You feed it oxygen, blowing across it. A super-quick thanks does the same: it blows oxygen across an ardent new donor, keeping that small flame alive, excited by your mission. Your vision. Your potential IN THEIR LIVES. At the very least, a super-quick thanks gets your organization past what often happens in the same 48-hour period: buyer's remorse.

Look, the standard for thanking in the nonprofit world has fallen so low that *any* unusual gratitude on your part will probably net you far more friends.

As The Agitator reported in 2013, "A three-minute thank-you phone call will boost first-year [donor] retention by 30%." In 2017, Leah Eustace at Good Works confirmed this phenomenon: "A one minute thank-you call to new donors (done by a telemarketing firm for $1/call), increased conversion by over 30%." In 2017, The Agitator chimed in again, with fresh data from America's public radio stations: "In its first year, the 'thank-you call' program generated 56% increase in first-year donor retention, 72% increase in first-year retention revenue."

Yet few organizations prioritize a new-donor phone thank-you program, despite the heavy expense of acquiring these first-time supporters. It's nuts. It should be in every fundraiser's job description: "You will manage an effective new-donor thank-you program."

The ghastly truth is that most charities thank poorly (if at all). They predictably, relentlessly, remorsefully, and (let's hope) unwittingly, UNDERwhelm their donors. Be the "OVERwhelmer" instead. Your charity will reap rich rewards.

"The key period is the first 90 days," Jay Love observes. He's the founder of Bloomerang, a donor management software firm focused on donor retention. "You want to have as many touches as possible."[1]

Elements of a great thank-you

Tammy Zonker is a development director and consultant with an astonishing record of success. This is her personal checklist of recommendations when writing and sending a thank-you letter:

- You've sent the letter promptly, within 72 hours or less of gift receipt.
- You've triple-checked that the name (and everything else) in the letter is spelled correctly. You've also included the gift amount and any restrictions the donor has specified.
- You've included a "grateful testimonial" quote, either from someone served or from someone in a position to know. ("As head of nurses, I can tell you quite honestly that your gift . . .")
- Your pronouns are about the donor, with a 3:1 ratio of "You" vs. "We."
- You're using phrasing that obeys what Jerry Panas calls the BOY rule: "Because of you . . ."
- You've included what Tammy calls "mission impact statements." These are evidence from the field that your programs work. Keep it short.
- The "best person" really has signed the letter. (In other words, if you were a donor, who would you like to hear from most? Maybe a mother whose child was saved? Or maybe you'd prefer the board chair?)
- You've included a handwritten personal message. For many readers, this will be the "warmth highlight" of the letter.[2]

---

1 Via Pam Grow, April 2017.

2 As presented by Tammy Zonker at the AFP International Fundraising Conference in San Francisco, April 2017.

Should I include an "ask" in my thanks?

Lisa Sargent, a specialist on thanking, says, as a rule, "never, ever, include an ask in a thank you. And never, ever, include a donation reply slip." She also says, however, "I reserve the right to change my mind based on results."

Jeff Brooks has *had* different results.

"We've found," he wrote in 2014, "that it's BEST to include a reply coupon in receipts (plus a return envelope). It dramatically increases response, which leads to better retention. The thing NOT to do is use standard ask techniques, like sad stories, negative photos, urgency, etc. The tenor of the package must be thankfulness and good news. You're talking to someone who really gets it, and is emotionally well positioned to give again."

Lisa continues to test her "never" premise, but so far it's held up with her clients. One of her clients *does* add a Business Reply Envelope to every thank-you, as a convenience if someone wishes to send a check. But there is no reply device with the envelope, nor does the thank-you letter ask for a gift.

Like Lisa, keep an open mind.

Angel Aloma, executive director at Food for the Poor, reports, "On average, we get more than one-fifth of our net income from direct mail from our thank you letters." Like Lisa, he does not make an ask in these letters, but he does include an envelope and a reply device.

But even Angel doesn't always include an ask. In 2012, he ran a test with 50,000 of that charity's top donors:

- 25,000 received an extra thank-you at the beginning of the year. This mailing was a simple expression of gratitude for past generosity. There was no ask or reply device included.
- 25,000 did NOT receive this extra thanks.

Twelve months later, Angel reviewed the results.

Both groups had given the same number of gifts. But, tantalizingly, the group that received the extra thank-you note was more generous. That group gave almost $450,000 more in total during the year than the group that did not receive the extra thank-you.

THANK YOU

Pat Bradley to you show details show image slideshow Dec 29 2016

Hi Tom
I hope your Christmas was special because if anyone deserves it, you surely do. Thank you for sending your emails imparting your wisdom to so many people.

Thank you for your generosity. Your donation is greatly appreciated and was used to help one of the girls in our Refuge home in Ethiopia. You made it possible for her to move into her own apartment and start her life of independence. She came from the red-light district and after one year in our home she graduated this month and will be moving to her own apartment early in Jan. This will be the first time in her life she has her "own place"!

Thanks for making this happen!

I was going to call and personally thank you but we do not have your number.

Please pass my gratitude to Simone and I pray 2017 is the best year for both of you, blessed with health, peace and prosperity beyond your wildest dreams.

Thank you for EVERYTHING!
Pat
PS. This girl is 19 years old and spent 5 years trapped in the red light district

Pat Bradley
Crisis Aid
1-888-740-7779
www.crisisaid.org

CRISIS AID® INTERNATIONAL

Emails with thanks in the subject line earn unusually high open rates, research shows. This high-touch example from Crisis Aid International thanks me seven times in one brief note, without any additional ask. It also tells me what my money helped do (move a 19-year-old girl into a Refuge Home after "5 years spent trapped in the red light district"), anticipating my need to know (which is good customer sevice). One of the most persistent complaints donors make in surveys: "I have no idea what they did with my money."

CHAPTER 23

Triggers

People give because something in your latest communication triggered a response. What was the trigger?

Emotional triggers

Master a modest handful of so-called "emotional triggers" . . . and you will master probably 95% of what you need to know to write effective fundraising appeals, donor newsletters, and the giving pages on your website.

These emotional triggers work because of preexisting factors in the typical human brain, so it doesn't matter whether they're delivered via print or digital (or in person, for that matter).

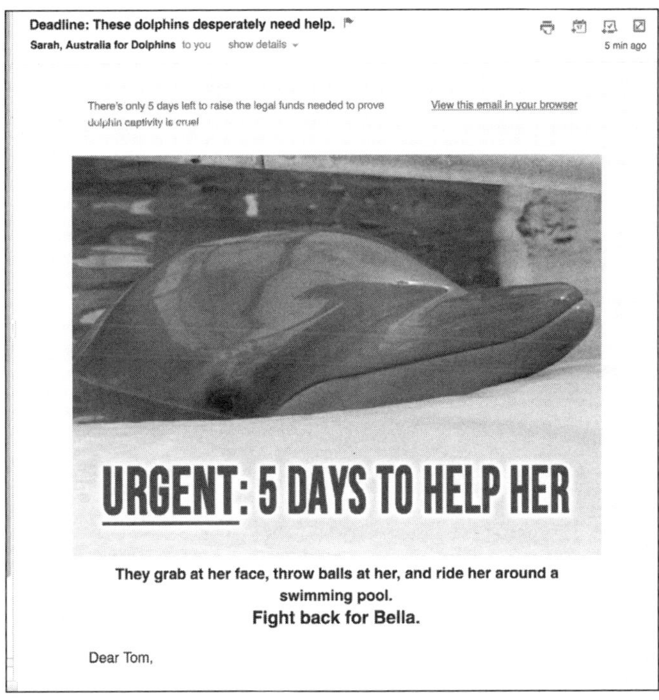

1. The subject line underscores urgency with two words: "deadline" and "desperately." Once opened, the email recaps the fight ("to prove dolphin captivity is cruel"); establishes eye contact with Bella, the victim; depicts her humiliating plight ("throw balls at her"); starts the countdown; and addresses me by name.

The biggies, cited often by direct mail experts, include these (in alpha order, not in order of potency):

- **Anger**—"How can you kill a dolphin? I'm furious about this. Why does stuff like that keep happening? I wish somebody would do something about it." Emphasizing urgency helps drive response in anger-based appeals. See Australia for Dolphins appeal below.
- **Duty**—"That's what people like me do." "I should . . ." "If I don't, who will?"

2. Throughout this long, illustrated email appeal, I'm repeatedly addressed by my name, in an attempt to make the fight personal, and given opportunities to act ("Please click here"). This passage emphasizes two offers: "a once-in-a-lifetime chance to put the global dolphin captivity industry under a microscope" and a dollar-for-dollar match.

- **Exclusivity**—"That would be a good group to join. I'd like to be one of them." Exclusivity offers include President's Circles ("Give $1,000 annually and . . .), legacy societies, special events.
- **Fear**—"Are my grandkids going to be able to breathe the air?"
- **Flattery**—"You said something very nice about me. You made me feel good. I'll do something nice back." A gift emerges.

- **Greed**—"I want to live in the best place on earth. But there are problems here, too. And I can do something to help." Call it "good greed" or maybe enlightened self-interest. Why do I give to my local volunteer fire department? Because they've already saved me twice.

Tom, dolphins like Bella desperately need your help. Will you chip in to reach the target in time?

Please click here to make an urgent donation - and have it doubled.

Right now captive dolphins like Bella are in a race against time, where every single dollar makes a really big difference. **If you chip in with a $20 donation it will automatically double to $40. And a $50 contribution immediately increases to a massive $100.**

People grope at Bella's face behind bars.

3. More personalization; another high-visibility chance to act and enraging descriptions like "People grope at Bella's face behind bars."

- **Guilt**—"I wish I hadn't done that." With that common thought is born a lifelong attachment to supporting a certain cause. Been there, done that.

- **Hope**—Donors buy hope. Hope is what you sell. Many, if not most, charities solve problems. In an industrialized world, nature needs lots of protection. Millions don't have clean drinking water. The arts struggle to survive. *Whatever the cause*, the charity sells **hope** that the situation can be remedied, fixed, ameliorated, changed, improved.

- **Salvation**—"We're all sinners." Doing good is the responsibility of all conscientious or devout people. There's a chance we can save ourselves from our base nature. There's a chance we can save others from their fates.

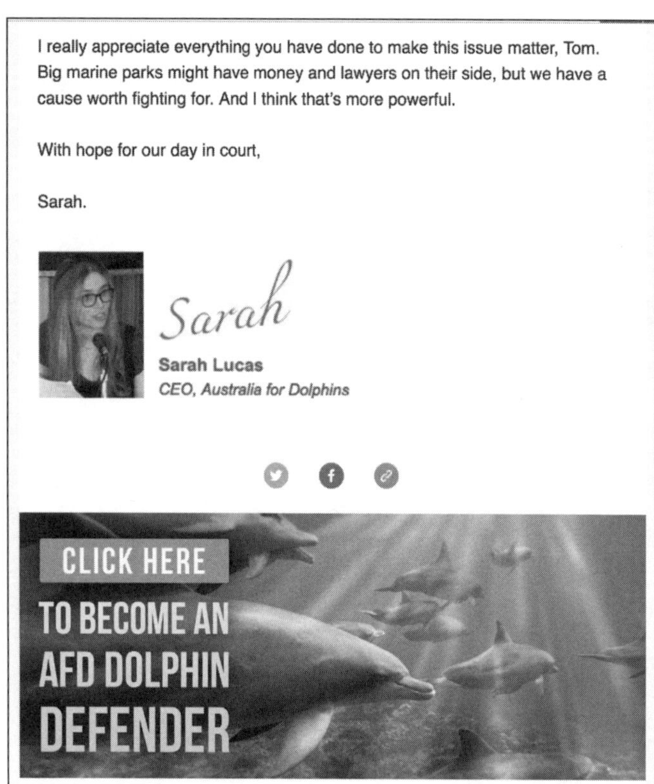
I really appreciate everything you have done to make this issue matter, Tom. Big marine parks might have money and lawyers on their side, but we have a cause worth fighting for. And I think that's more powerful.

With hope for our day in court,

Sarah.

Sarah

Sarah Lucas
CEO, Australia for Dolphins

4. More personalization; a moral challenge ("Big marine parks might have money and lawyers on their side, but we have a cause worth fighting for"); a closing expression of hope from CEO Sarah, who's shown, establishing a person-to-person contact and a final call to action asking me to take on the superhero role of Dolphin Defender. Creative: Pareto, Australia.

Dr. Cialdini's behavioral triggers

Robert B. Cialdini is the author of the bestseller *Influence*. "In the field of influence and persuasion, he is the most cited social psychologist in the world today," his publisher says. He is the Regents' Professor Emeritus of Psychology and Marketing at Arizona State University.

He researched and established "six key principles of influence." These are the factors that cause people to act.

1. **Reciprocity**—People tend to return a favor. If I give you something, you feel obliged to give me something back. Why do people *still* make gifts when charities send yet more uninvited, unneeded, unwanted self-sticking address labels? Reciprocity. Why does "grateful patient" fundraising work? Reciprocity.

2. **Commitment**—"I pledge my support for the next five years." We honor what we commit to; to do otherwise threatens our self-image. Or as Wikipedia has it: "If people commit, orally or in writing, to an idea or goal, they are more likely to honor that commitment because of establishing that idea or goal as being congruent with their self-image." Joining a legacy society is commitment.

3. **Liking**—If I like you, I'm more likely to buy from you. If I like a charity, I'm more likely to give to it. Street fundraising (or what's called face-to-face fundraising in Australia and derogatorily "chugging" in the UK press) relies on liking.
4. **Social proof**—"Why do I give? Because people like me do things like that." We copy the behavior of people we admire or identify with. "Did a donor like me also leave a gift in her will? Maybe I should consider doing that, too." That's social proof.
5. **Authority**—People tend to obey authority figures. When I wrote a matching-gift appeal for a Catholic high school, I said, "Get me a priest." The good father didn't write the letter. He didn't approve the letter. He was needed to sign the letter. We needed his title and his voice asking for the matching gifts. It was a huge success. Another huge success was a hospice appeal signed by a doctor whose wife died in hospice care.
6. **Scarcity**—"Limited time only." A perception of scarcity creates demand. Research shows that those classic campaign thermometers work better in the late stages to drive in gifts, when you're closing in on 90% of your goal. Why? Maybe because people feel the pressure to jump into something they care about (like a church restore the steeple drive) before time runs out.

The cuteness factor

Puppies, kittens and kids. They have one thing in common: humans think they're cute. But why *is* that?

Biology.

I've heard many fundraisers make a complaint along these lines: "Our organization is about policy issues. Economics, politics. We don't serve cute kids. That makes it much harder to find donors."

They're not wrong.

Nature has built into humans an automatic positive response to young faces. From Wikipedia's well-sourced article on the topic: "Konrad Lorenz argued in 1949 that infantile features triggered nurturing responses in adults and that this was an evolutionary adaptation which helped ensure that adults cared for their children, ultimately securing the survival of the species. Some later scientific studies have provided further evidence for Lorenz's theory." Lorenz, a 1973 Nobel Laureate for his research into instinctive behavior, wrote, "Humans feel affection for animals with juvenile features: large eyes, bulging craniums, retreating chins."

If you have cuteness, use it. It's a reliable trigger. If your charity is about economic policy, maybe you should include a photo of a puppy reading your latest white paper.

Meet Dr. Gwen Moss,
member since 2005 of the Legacy Society
for Hampton Roads

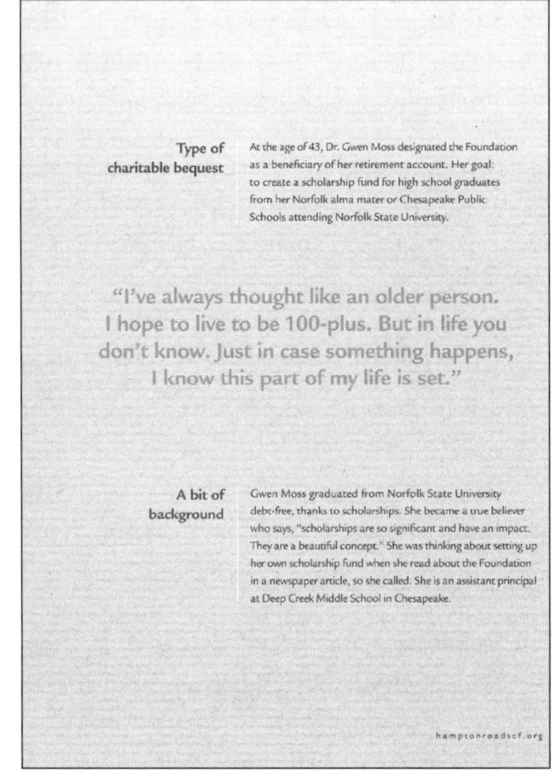

Type of charitable bequest

At the age of 43, Dr. Gwen Moss designated the Foundation as a beneficiary of her retirement account. Her goal: to create a scholarship fund for high school graduates from her Norfolk alma mater or Chesapeake Public Schools attending Norfolk State University.

"I've always thought like an older person. I hope to live to be 100-plus. But in life you don't know. Just in case something happens, I know this part of my life is set."

A bit of background

Gwen Moss graduated from Norfolk State University debt-free, thanks to scholarships. She became a true believer who says, "scholarships are so significant and have an impact. They are a beautiful concept." She was thinking about setting up her own scholarship fund when she read about the Foundation in a newspaper article, so she called. She is an assistant principal at Deep Creek Middle School in Chesapeake.

hamptonroadscf.org

Meet Dr. Tim Bostic and Tony London,
members since 2007 of the Legacy Society
for Hampton Roads

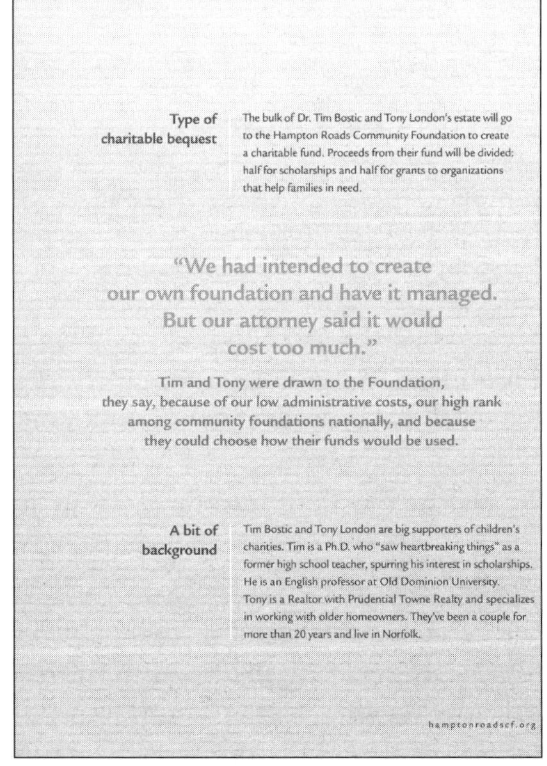

Type of charitable bequest

The bulk of Dr. Tim Bostic and Tony London's estate will go to the Hampton Roads Community Foundation to create a charitable fund. Proceeds from their fund will be divided: half for scholarships and half for grants to organizations that help families in need.

"We had intended to create our own foundation and have it managed. But our attorney said it would cost too much."

Tim and Tony were drawn to the Foundation, they say, because of our low administrative costs, our high rank among community foundations nationally, and because they could choose how their funds would be used.

A bit of background

Tim Bostic and Tony London are big supporters of children's charities. Tim is a Ph.D. who "saw heartbreaking things" as a former high school teacher, spurring his interest in scholarships. He is an English professor at Old Dominion University. Tony is a Realtor with Prudential Towne Realty and specializes in working with older homeowners. They've been a couple for more than 20 years and live in Norfolk.

hamptonroadscf.org

What Dr. Cialdini's "social proof" looks like. There were in total five brief photo-bios selected as "social proof" for this community foundation pamphlet promoting charitable bequests. Research showed that people commonly assumed only the rich leave charitable bequests. In fact, middle-class estates in North America (i.e., those without professional estate planners) leave by far the largest number of bequests for charity. Dr. Gwen Moss, school principal, is representative. She's a respected professional, like many bequestors. And then there's this fact: households without heirs are most likely to leave a charitable bequest. Tim Bostic and Tony London were married on May 2, 2015. They'd met 26 years earlier at a country-western dance class. They have no kids. But they've always been caring, compassionate, community-minded people. So they put charity in their wills. Stuart Levy lost his wife. "I have no children and no immediate family." But he has a friend whose life was changed by a scholarship. So he added an endowed scholarship fund to his will.

CHAPTER 24

Interest me (or else)

Let us now praise extraordinary insights, this one courtesy of Howard Luck Gossage (1917–1969). "A man who hated advertising," it's said. Yet he was inducted into the Advertising Copywriters Hall of Fame.

Celebrated ad pioneer David Ogilvy called Gossage "the most articulate rebel in the advertising business," a man who felt "advertising was too valuable . . . to waste on commercial products . . . that it justified its existence only when it was used for social purposes."

I.e., for good causes.

Here's what the very estimable Mr. Gossage had to say: "The real fact of the matter is that nobody reads ads. People read what interests them, and sometimes it's an ad."

And sometimes it's your direct mail solicitation . . . or the cover story on your donor newsletter . . . or that email alert your organization just sent.

In each case the decision to read or not to read your stuff will come down to one thing: *Is a person interested in what you're saying and/or showing?*

Since this is a vitally important principle, let me repeat.

Your donors and prospects are under no obligation to pay attention. If you don't somehow interest them, they won't read what you send.

Basic psychology: what interests me most is *me*. Ask anyone. We add a chapter to our life's story every day.

My gifts, my acts of charity, have a supporting, even a leading, role in that unspooling, personal, no-one-can-predict-the-outcome story.

How to interest people: A checklist

So, how *do* you interest people? Here's a checklist of some things I consider when I write for donors or prospects:

Am I being "donor-centric" enough?

- Have I said what amazing things the organization could do with their gifts? Did I mention worthwhile results from previous gifts?

- Did I celebrate the donor LOUDLY as the hero? (In other words, did I say in some fashion over and over, "This good work would not be possible without your help.")
- Did I talk about the organization's cost efficiency? (In surveys, donors often say that they believe charities are poorly run. Let's build trust, people!)

Am I taking advantage of human psychology?

- Am I telling (*and* showing) people things they DON'T know? Does my information have news value? Is it unique or innovative? Are my photos surprising in some way? (Not bland, predictable or boring.)
- Is it bold, passionate? (Not bland, predictable or boring.)
- Am I aiming for the heart? Have I included plenty of emotional triggers? (Fear, anger, greed, exclusivity, scarcity.)
- Do I use the word "you" often?
- Is the overall tone conversational rather than formal?
- Am I making it easy for skimmers, flippers and browsers to glean information? If, for instance, someone reads just the headlines, will the person still understand my key messages?
- Is the publication as a whole a quick read? Am I writing short sentences? Am I using action verbs? Have I eliminated jargon?
- Am I using anecdotes to illuminate our most pressing issues? The human brain is hard-wired by evolution to understand narrative.
- Am I using my statistical evidence like a spear, to make a single important point?
- Can I use testimonials anywhere, to inspire the faithful and calm the doubters?
- Have I made at least one offer they can respond to immediately? People want to act NOW!

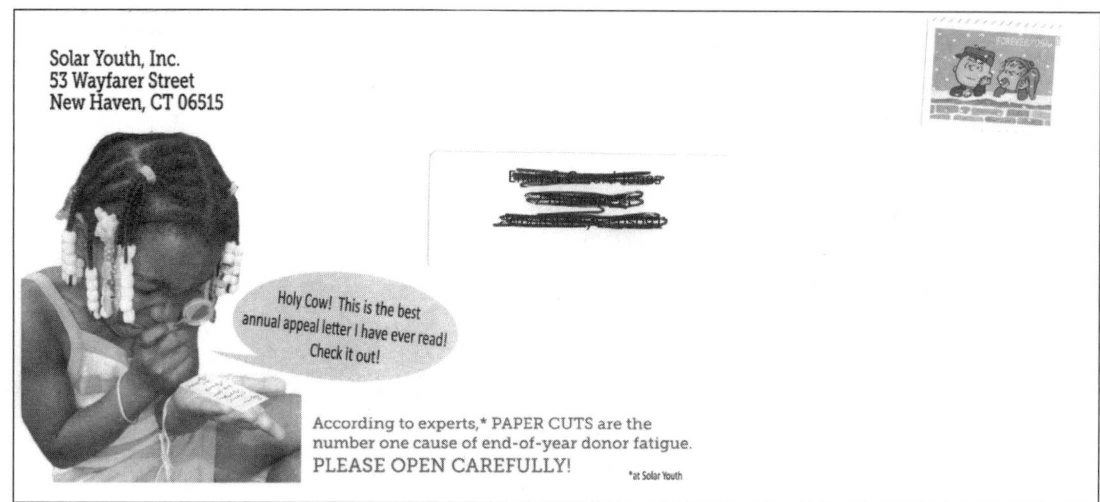

Yes! I want to be a FOSY!

(Friend of Solar Youth)

- ❍ I'm a **Frequent FOSY** and would like to make a monthly gift of ______/month!
- ❍ I'm all about helping New Haven's youth achieve nothing less than lifelong success and will invest _________this year!
- ❍ I'm a **SUPER FOSY** and want to discuss making a long term major gift. Contact me!
- ❍ I'm an **Investing FOSY** and want you to contact me about donating stocks.
- ❍ I'm a **Lifelong FOSY** and have included Solar Youth in my will.

Your donation is tax deductible to the full extent of the law.

Ways to pay!

Visit us ONLINE at www.solaryouth.org/donate, or...

Name ______________________

Address ______________________

____

City/State/Zip ______________________

Email ______________________

Phone ______________________

❍ I have enclosed a check, we're good to go!

❍ Credit Card (MC, Amex, VISA, Discover)

Name as it appears on card:

____

Number______________________

Exp. Date_________ Security Code___________

Check here if you DO NOT want your name shared on our public donor list ❍

Is this envelope bland, predictable, inoffensive, safe, and just like all the others? No way! This charming appeal from New Haven's Solar Youth ("empowering youth to achieve lifelong success") made me beam as soon as I picked it up. That's how great donor relationships sometimes start: with a moment of surprise and delight. The FOSY reply device continues the fun, establishing a warm, enjoyable personality for this nonprofit founded in 2000.

CHAPTER 25

(1) emotions (2) totally (3) rule

In a contest between two competent appeals from the same charity, one that's "well reasoned" vs. one that's packed with emotional hooks . . . well, it's not even a contest, really.

The *emotional* appeal will outperform the *rational* appeal by many multiples. Every time. Guaranteed. It's the way our brains are wired.

With the advent of Functional MRIs and other investigative tools in the late 20th century, neuroscientists were finally able to directly observe a phenomenon they'd suspected for more than a century: the dominance of emotion in human decision-making.

As USC neuroscientist Dr. Antoine Bechara sums it up, "There is a popular notion, which most of us learn from early on in life, that logical, rational calculation forms the basis of sound decisions. Many people say, 'emotion has no IQ'; emotion can only cloud the mind and interfere with good judgment. But . . . these notions [are] wrong and [have] no scientific basis." Instead, "decision-making is a process guided by emotions."

As the *New York Times* reported in 2007, "A bevy of experiments in recent years suggest that the conscious mind is like a monkey riding a tiger of subconscious decisions and actions in progress, frantically making up stories about being in control."

"I'm different"

Making a gift to charity is like any other purchase decision.

But not quite.

A gift to charity is a transaction with a mystery built in. I give you my hard-earned money. You give me what, exactly? An oil change? A sandwich? It starts like a transaction . . . but then what?

Nothing concrete.

Yes, each time I make a gift (neuroscience confirms), I experience in my skull a quick squirt of a pleasure compound. (Dopamine, maybe?)

But that quick spurt is probably ***all*** I'm going to get from you, lover . . . because analytical minds on your board and CEO-level tend to see me as a number filed in a database . . . *not* as the complex psychology I actually am, with many different needs.

As you would guess, disappointment is built in.

Still, expecting almost nothing, I do faithfully, guiltily, humbly, dutifully write my check to your appeal (or go online to make my gift), signifying YES!

YES! I AM your supporter.

I AM your NEW supporter.

Which makes me different from every other person on Planet Earth. Then comes your next opportunity, served on a plate you should avoid touching. ("Careful, that's very hot!")

"You know what people want more than anything?" superstar marketer Seth Godin reminds us. "They want to be missed."

You can do that, right?

You've planned for that, right?

Behind every decision to make a gift . . .

. . . stands the real me!

My values.

My upbringing.

My life experiences, maybe more bad than good.

My guilt.

My failures.

My powerlessness.

My hate.

My fear.

My desires.

My love.

My hope.

My beliefs.

My wonder.

My humility.

My identity altogether, finally, at the end, when I stop walking: what's left when I face myself in the mirror.

Poor lovers, most of you

When I make a first gift to some new charity, I certainly *hope* that nonprofit will prolong the chemical pleasure I feel when I am in a philanthropic mood.

Philanthropic mood? Happens a few times a day on average. None of what follows is kidding: as a donor, I enjoy low lighting. Relaxing clothes. A quick shower. And a serious drink.

Fundraising is a tool

Philanthropy is as nature intended.

Helping others is in our heads. We are a social species. We have some common brain threads and impulses.

When you give *anything* to a vulnerable person—whether it's directions on the street or a week of meals to a hungry homeless family or your volunteer time—you *feel good*. That's biology. Your brain feels a warm glow when you donate.

Fundraisers have talked about the warm glow for a long time. At first it was a likely theory. Now science says that these early fundraising hypothesizers were absolutely right: the "warm glow" is real.

More important, it's measurable.

The human animal emotionally, biologically, devotedly, physically, thanks to chemistry *enjoys* giving.

Are charities in the go-away business? Sometimes you wonder

I don't expect much from those new charities I support.

As my base income grew, after two decades of ever-heavier earning, I gave to more and more. I didn't have kids. I had a reassuring retirement fund socked away. I could afford some occasional gifts to charities that made me feel better.

I quickly saw that most nonprofits were lousy at prolonging my pleasure. "Here's all I want from you," I finally wrote. "Tell me I'm a reasonably good person. Don't go crazy. But just tell me that my help matters."

Since we're being honest, here's my secret opinion: most charities I've honored with a gift were hesitant, indifferent, negligent, uncouth, rude, demanding, stiff, formal, and/or cold.

Poor lovers get replaced quickly.

GIVING is a fairly *irrational* act, prompted by empathy, desire, pleasure, anger, and a host of other emotions. Psychologists have delineated more than 100 states in the human emotional pantry.

But emotion is really all you have. Reason doesn't lead directly to action, science found. Neurological researcher Donald B. Calne explains it this way: "The essential difference between emotion and reason is that emotion leads to action while reason leads to conclusions."

In other words, reasoning gets me *thinking*. Thinking, though, is *not* action. It's your ability to touch my emotions that gets me past my native inertia and gets me *giving*. That's why you always lead with emotion in appeals to individual donors . . . and trail with reason. Not the reverse.

Data kills interest on contact. Data is poison to non-specialists.

Tina Cincotti summed up the science nicely. "People act because you moved them emotionally—you made them feel something. MRIs show that it's our brain's emotional nerve center that gets activated first. It's not a rational, logical process where we weigh costs against benefits and make an informed decision. Your brain gets involved later, largely as a rubber stamp to make sure you don't do anything too wacky! But it starts with the heart. If you're not hitting your donors on an emotional level, then you're not raising as much money as you could."

Seth Godin agrees. "Marketers don't convince. Engineers convince. Marketers persuade. Persuasion appeals to the emotions and to fear and to the imagination. Convincing requires a spreadsheet or some other rational device. If you're spending a lot of your time trying to convince people, it's no wonder it's not working."

The last word goes to Paul Slovic, a prominent psychologist. His research into "psychic numbing" found that big numbers tend to reduce response: not as many act.

Slovic wrote,[3] "Most people are caring and will exert great effort to rescue individual victims whose needy plight comes to their attention. These same good people, however, often become numbly indifferent to the plight of individuals who are 'one of many.'"

Why does this occur? He concluded, "The reported numbers of deaths represent dry statistics, 'human beings with the tears dried off,' that fail to spark emotion or feeling and thus fail to motivate action."

When you communicate with individual donors—whether it's in your appeals, newsletters, website, emails, Facebook postings—avoid stats and embrace stories. Jeff Brooks writing in Future Fundraising Now, January 12, 2016, says: "Here are some common mistakes [adopted from PhilanTopic] that drain emotion from messages:

Mistakenly assume that every person is an expert.
Ignore the emotional appeal of their brand.
Put too much emphasis on the "investment."
Tries to sell an idea instead of impact.

Here are some others that I often encounter:

3 Paul Slovic, *Judgment and Decision Making*, April 2007.

You think you can instruct people into caring.
You think emotion is somehow dishonestly manipulative.
Your primary goal is to feel good about what you say and how you say it.
"Dignity" is extremely important to you.
Political correctness.

Jeff concludes: "Fundraising that works is emotional. It's simplistic, blatant, corny, and soupy. That's just the way it is. There's nothing wrong with your donors. That's just the playground you're playing on when you do fundraising."

You will encounter staff who feel that "simplistic, blatant, corny, and soupy" fundraising is the low road. They're wrong. Their untrained opinions are irrelevant and may be dangerous to your bottom line.

Get as many emotional moments into your giving communications as you can. Interest in advocacy groups such as the Center for Constitutional Rights is fueled by outrage. CCR's "donate" button takes no special advantage of that, but it could, by adding just one word. See DONATE button in lower image.

CHAPTER 26

You're an intrusion, too

Every day thousands of messages head for your eyes and ears, aiming to reach your heart and mind. It's a well-funded total assault . . . via web, TV, radio, newspapers, magazines, roadside advertising, faxes, flyers pinned to bulletin boards, bumper stickers, labels on bottles and cans . . . and, even more personally, mail, email, and phone.

You are besieged by voices eager to get a piece of you: your time, your loyalty, your attention, your money.

Is it any wonder your defenses are up?

So you sort the incoming into three piles:

1. Stuff you can't ignore because, if you do, something bad will happen. (Bills, a jury duty summons, an email from your mom.)
2. Stuff you *can* safely ignore and *nothing* bad will happen. (Pretty much everything else.)
3. And a little bit of stuff that especially interests you.

Nonprofit communications don't enjoy any special exemptions. Your materials, particularly your fundraising materials, are part of the onslaught. You are an intrusion, headed for pile #2. Every item your organization sends is guilty until proven innocent.

Guilty of what? Guilty of wasting the reader's time with material that serves *your* purpose (to raise money) . . . but doesn't interest or reward the reader.

Be pessimistic when communicating to prospects and supporters. *Don't* expect good results. Sure, it's a paradox. But it works in your favor. The less optimistic you are, the more you achieve. (Promise.) The people who take lots for granted chronically underperform.

The people who take *nothing* for granted succeed beyond their way-too-modest expectations.

We're losing to the goldfish

Goldfish now have a longer attention span than humans. Truth, not fiction: science measures these things.

Goldfish will pay attention for 10 seconds on average, researchers reported in 2013. Humans that same year could only manage 8 seconds.

Our attention spans used to be longer. But onslaughts of email . . . omnipresent clickable advertising . . . pinging smart phones . . . Twitter and the ilk: together, they're turning the ability to concentrate into a thing of the past.

Research reported by Multiview in 2016 found that "we check our smartphones an average of 46 times a day—a 40 percent increase from just two years ago." Is this cause for alarm? No. It's cause for consideration.

We're heading ever deeper into the Age of Constant Distraction. You can't fight it. You have to work with it.

CHAPTER 27

The rise of skimming

These days, it's safest to assume that everyone's a skimmer, not a deep reader.

The Poynter Institute, a think tank and education provider serving the news industry, has repeatedly studied the reading behavior of average people. The key discovery: *People tend to skip the articles*, even those in professionally written news publications.

We look at the pictures mostly. (You're not surprised, are you?) More than half of us look at the headlines, too (i.e., the biggest type). About a third look at captions and anything brief (the short, easy stuff).

And 8 out of 10 of us never penetrate beyond the opening paragraph of any article. The loneliest place on the planet is paragraph three. Almost no one visits.

For organizations with many important things to write about, this reality has to hurt. But our propensity toward skimming has advantages—and implications—in donor communications.

- **One advantage:** reducing costs.

  Why, for instance, print a 12-page newsletter filled with long articles when a 4-page newsletter filled with short ones would actually be welcomed far more . . . and almost certainly generate more gifts?

- **A serious implication:** getting your message across.

  If your goal is to convince donors that they play an important role in your mission, do NOT bury that message at the end of an article no one is likely to read.

  I've seen this mistake countless times. The charity runs an article about some program . . . and then, at the very end of that article, conspicuously thanks donors for making that program possible. Was anyone still reading? Most had stopped long before.

Was reading ever really the point?

We use words to raise money. It's reasonable to assume, therefore, that communications are somehow about getting people to read.

No.

Fundraising communications are about getting people to ACT . . . if not immediately, then sooner or later.

Reading is optional.

Look at it another way. Which would you rather have, if you could only choose from these two options:

- Someone who reads your stuff but never responds?
- Or someone who *doesn't* read your stuff but sends you a gift anyway?

Obviously, you'd choose the latter, as would anyone with a dollar goal to make. It's not ideal. But it pays the bills.

I bring up the distinction between reading and acting for an important reason having to do with your workload: to release you from the burden of worrying so much about writing newsletter articles, white papers, and other longer prose pieces.

The reality is, people will read very little of what you send them. They don't have time in their busy, complex lives. And most nonprofit communications aren't sufficiently interesting to win devoted readers, anyway. (Sorry!)

The bald fact that they don't read your stuff doesn't mean they don't love you, incidentally.

If the people on the receiving end are donors, they *do* love you (well, they *like* you anyway). But they're time-challenged and fiercely assaulted each day by thousands of other messages.

Into the Weeds

CHAPTER 28

AIDA (it's not an opera, it's a sales approach)

There's a well-worn sales formula that advertisers have relied on probably since the Phoenicians: A-I-D-A. The AIDA acronym describes this sequence: Attention, Interest, Desire, Action.

1. You (the advertiser) try to grab my *attention*. (Anything goes. *"Yoo-hoo?"* **BANG!** Goal #1 for consumer ads is to interrupt you and hijack your attention. Dropping a steel pot lid on a tile floor is the level of subtlety you can expect. **MADE YOU LOOK!** Now you know why TV ads are so loud, obnoxious, desperate to entertain.)
2. You hook my *interest.* (You say stuff that I like, enjoy or surprises me.)
3. You stir my *desire.* (You show me how your product or service will benefit me: promising why it will make me happier, more successful, more attractive, taller, smarter, less of a failure.)
4. You make it easy to *act*: to buy your product or service.

AIDA in the fundraising world

The AIDA formula describes the typical journey a consumer might take on her rambling way toward a purchase decision—i.e., the point at which she forks over her hard-earned money to a cashier or online.

Donations are purchase decisions, too.

Your donors-to-come will sometimes follow the same AIDA path . . . but with a significant twist at the end.

1. You attempt to grab my **attention**.
2. You hook my **interest**.

3. You stir my **desire**. You're not selling me soap. You have to connect . . . with my unique values, emotions, personal interests, experiences and such. Reread the chapter about the donor's brain if you need a refresher. **You give me an important job to do.** You ask me to fix a child's cleft palate or bring clean water to a thirsty, suffering village. You invite me join an advocacy group devoted to a single worthy goal. You invite me to take up a fight worth fighting. You give me hope that something I worry about can be fixed. You reduce my anger. You validate my self-image as a caring person. You give me a way to pay back for a blessed life. You give me a way to live out the teachings of Jesus Christ or Mohammad or the Buddha or Confucius. You give me a way to repent for my mistakes. You offer me a purpose. The sale is made at this stage, by the way. From this point on, it's just a matter of making the purchase (i.e., making the gift) easy.

4. Finally, you call me to **action**. Here's where the twist comes in: I get nothing tangible in return. So, what can you give me in exchange for my gift? Emotional gratification. Everyone likes emotional gratification. And that gratification starts immediately, if you're any good at this.

Get my attention. Get me reading. This case for support starts its story with a deceptively unthreatening statement on the cover. Once the reader's been lured inside, a harrowing tale unfolds of an infant in danger, illustrating the need for best-in-class neonatal facilities. Creative by Maggie Cohn and Andrea Hopkins.

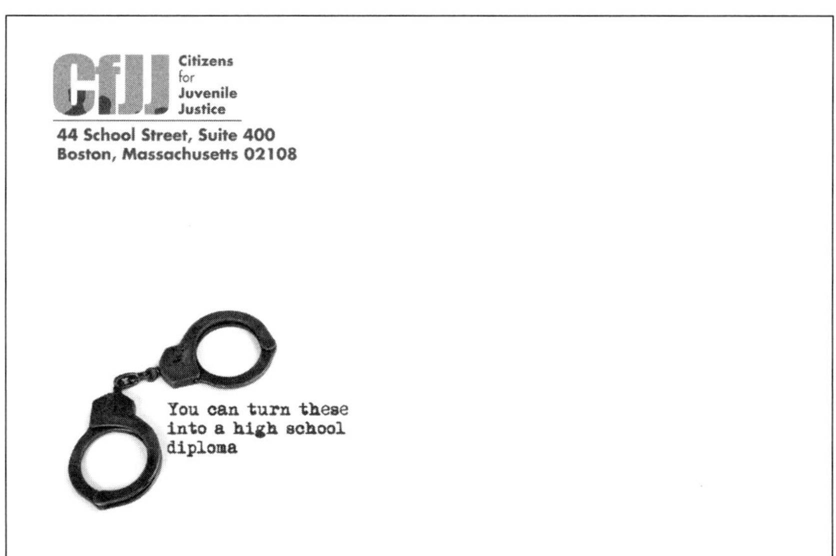

When I first saw this envelope, I had a one-word response: "Wow!" That's the "A" in the AIDA formula. Written by Tina Cincotti, Funding Change Consulting, with design by Wendy Brovold, this successful direct mail pack doesn't beat around the bush: it offers the potential donor a big job right on the envelope. World-class direct mail guru Jerry Huntsinger says this about that, **"The outer/carrier envelope:** the purpose is to get it ripped open with as much anticipation as possible. Nothing else." For those of you doing an email solicitation, Huntsinger's dictum goes like this, **"The subject line:** the purpose is to get the email opened with as much anticipation as possible. Nothing else."

CHAPTER 29

Stories, not stats

Some funding sources *want* stats, *need* stats, and have the paid staff to correctly interpret your stats: governments and big foundations.

For individual donors, though, it's a very different story. Let's get a little technical. Here's Professor Paul J. Zak writing in the *Harvard Business Review*, in an October 28, 2014, article titled "Why Your Brain Loves Good Storytelling":

> Many business people have already discovered the power of storytelling in a practical sense—they have observed how compelling a well-constructed narrative can be. But recent scientific work is putting a much finer point on just how stories change our attitudes, beliefs, and behaviors. . . .
>
> By taking blood draws before and after the narrative, we found that character-driven stories do consistently cause oxytocin synthesis. [Oxytocin is a neurochemical that motivates us to cooperate.] Further, the amount of oxytocin released by the brain predicted how much people were willing to help others; for example, donating money to a charity associated with the narrative.

Stories do that. Statistics don't.

In fact, according to the laboratory, the whole "statistics vs. stories" debate is pointless. And yet it's harder to kill than an urban myth such as "you can see the Great Wall of China from space." (You really can't.)

To many, it seems so obvious: "Some people like stories. Some people like numbers."

Stories, numbers: even-steven. But even-steven is not true with individual donors.

Correctly, it should be stated: "ALL individual donors like stories"—there's feel-good neurochemistry involved, after all; dopamine-like stuff—"and a few individual donors like numbers as well as stories."

That's the brain's true state. Storytelling—narrative, if you prefer a fancier name—is universal. It has been more important to human evolution than opposable thumbs, as Lisa Cron points out in her excellent book, *Wired for Story: The Writer's Guide to Using Brain Science to Hook Readers from the Very First Sentence.*

Story: it is how we learn most of what we know.

Is your "trophy number" big in *my* eyes?

I backed into the nonprofit world.

Came from a high-tech, high-pressure commercial world. For five years, I dedicated every ounce of my professional life to a firm where 12-hour days were quite common and sleeping at the office was expected, if necessary. There, I helped a young technology firm founded by three hard drivers compete for contracts worth hundreds of millions of dollars . . . each.

In that environment I quickly lost my fear of very large numbers; one does. Big numbers were the norm, unintimidating. So now you, charity, come to me, pleading at the top of your voice. "There are 1,532 families."

I instantly react. But not the way you'd want. Because I'm thinking, judging from my experience: *Doesn't sound so bad.*

I'm wrong, of course. But my special, peculiar, personal, *you had no idea* context re: big numbers established my expectations for a lifetime. Bottom line: do NOT assume that what your organization thinks of as a crisis number will seem all that urgent to outsiders. Sure: they might share your passion. But will they share your context?

<Date, 2016>

<Addressee>
<Address1>
<Address2>
<City> <Province> <Postal>

Dear <Salutation>,

With Huntington disease, you always feel like you're 10 steps behind. You go from one intense moment to the next, and you never know what symptoms you'll deal with on any one day. But I feel like the Society is 10 steps ahead. Social workers can anticipate what I might need next and that makes me feel empowered, and in more control. –Jenna

You are the reason Jenna feels like we are 10 steps ahead.

Donors like you are with us every single day, providing direct services to families dealing with HD, and taking steps every day towards the next research breakthrough. Thank you!

Today, I'm writing to share with you some recent accomplishments, made possible because of your support, and to look ahead with you to the next crucial steps in our work.

<Salutation>, can we count on you to step up and stand together with us once again? Your special gift today of <Ask1>, <Ask2>, or <Ask3> would be a vital contribution to our cause. Your gift will go to work right away in your community and across Canada, helping families and funding critical research.

Your gift today will also be counted towards our new *Believe* campaign. We have a bold and ambitious goal to make a major investment in research and access to services, and this campaign reflects our shared belief that we can transform tomorrow together.

151 Frederick Street, Suite 400, Kitchener, ON N2H 2M2
1-800-998-7398 • info@huntingtonsociety.ca • www.huntingtonsociety.ca

This multi-piece direct mail package is storytelling brought to a high level by Jen Love and John Lepp, Agents for Good co-founders. Note how Jenna's story of her mother's diagnosis and struggle are woven through the letter and the timeline. Also note the heavy degree of donor-centricity throughout.

Here's what we'll do with your gift today:

Invest in Research. Recently, we have funded some of the most promising research in our history. For the first time, we have seen that it is possible not only to stop the disease from getting worse, but to reverse it (in a mouse model). Our investment strategy going forward will build on this, finding new treatments more quickly.

Supporting our Families. Everyone affected by HD deserves to have services and clinical trials accessible to them. Your support will help us reach out to families in rural and diverse communities. And you'll also help us expand our services for youth.

This brings me back to Jenna's story. Here, she beautifully captures a fundamentally important truth:

With Huntington disease, you're in a perpetual state of grief. My mom is not the same person she was when I was growing up. And when I notice little changes, little losses, I grieve a little bit more. It's heart wrenching—what lies ahead is so hard. Her care falls to my immediate family, so I have to be informed, knowledgeable and connected to others who can help me.

You can help us stay 10 steps ahead for Jenna and her family, and all our families, every single day. Jenna knows that as her mom's condition worsens, Jenna will be her voice and her main source of support. Our youth, like Jenna, need immediate help today, and will need our ongoing support in the future.

You can read more about what you helped achieve, and more about our *Believe* campaign, on the enclosed note. You'll also find enclosed a reply form you can use to make your gift today.

Please, help us stay 10 steps ahead and support our *Believe* campaign with your gift today.

Warm regards,

Bev Heim-Myers
Chief Executive Officer

P.S. You can show that you *Believe* and can transform tomorrow together by making your special gift today. Thank you!

FPO
FSC

Huntington Society of Canada
HUNTINGTON
Société Huntington du Canada

timeline

1973 Huntington Society of Canada is founded by Ralph and Ariel Walker

Thanks for letting me share some of my memories with you - Jenna

1983 Canadian scientist announces a marker linked to the HD gene, leading to a predictive test

1984: I'm born! Of course, I had no idea just how much HD would become part of my life...

1993: What a relief for families, to finally have a way to know for sure what's happening with your loved one.

1993 HD gene is discovered! Direct testing becomes available to families

1996 Canadian researchers stop the progression of HD in a mouse

2004: Looking back, I can't pinpoint exactly when mom's symptoms started, but around here we first started asking our family doctor.

2008: Mom's symptoms continue to worsen. In my heart, I know something is really wrong with her. But our family doctor keeps brushing it off.

2011 Discovery of a link between Alzheimer's disease and HD leads to increased scientific collaboration

2012 Researchers reverse HD symptoms in a mouse

2012: HD, in a mouse model, can not only be slowed but stopped and reversed! AMAZING!

2013: I found the society's website and self-diagnosed my mom. I called the number on the website and was immediately connected to a social worker who spent hours coaching me through the process of getting mom what she needs.

2013 Discovery that huntingtin protein bends differently than the protein from a normal gene and proves the normal shape can be restored

more →

2013: Our family doctor refuses to make a referral to the HD clinic. I was furious. But the HSC social workers contacted the clinic directly and got us in.

2013

2013 Youth Mentorship program established, making HSC a world leader in supporting young people affected by HD

2013: Mom's diagnosis confirmed. A crushing blow for our family.

2013: Social workers become part of our daily life. They are with us every step. I don't know what I would do without them.

2013: Mom becomes part of our local HD clinic. Immediate, positive change in her.

2014: Mom's treatments addressing symptoms are clearly working. We are constantly alert, watching for and talking about changes. But she's managing her symptoms better.

2015 5 clinical trials launched, first human trials addressing the root cause of HD. HSC launches a map locator, so families can easily find where the trials are located and how to get involved

2015

2015: My daughter Rose is born! I look at my beautiful baby and my heart aches for what's to come for our family. But I'm also completely committed to ending HD for her!

2015: The Youth Program is so important to me. I've found lifelong friends and we know what each other is going through. I am so grateful to find this necessary support system.

2016: The Society supports our family, locating a day program for mom.

2016

2016 Research investment to fund virtual networks that connect clinicians, scientists and patients, expediting discovery research to the HD community

2016: I share my story to inspire more caring people to join us and help families like mine. Every single gift helps!

Your support today means more hope for families like mine. Please, give today! – Jenna

CHAPTER 30

The Gift of Joy *(faster!)*

I invented a term: the Gift of Joy.

Feel free to call it whatever you choose to . . . so long as you know about it and practice delivering the Gift of Joy frequently and in high-visibility ways—all over your communications, digital, print and person to person.

What *is* this Gift of Joy?

Well, it's a special dab of love from you, the charity, applied directly to your donor's self-image. It's where you come right out and say, "Dear Donor, you're a wonderful person."

Three things characterize a Gift of Joy:

- You see it right away. It's easy to spot. Seconds count.
- It's personal, using the word *you* intimately.
- It credits the donor with making a real difference.

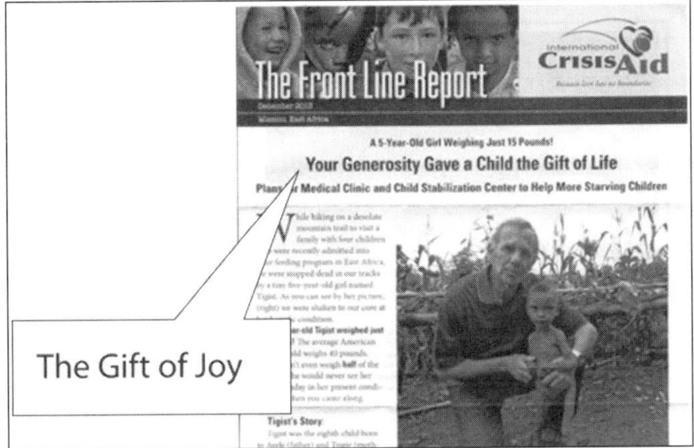

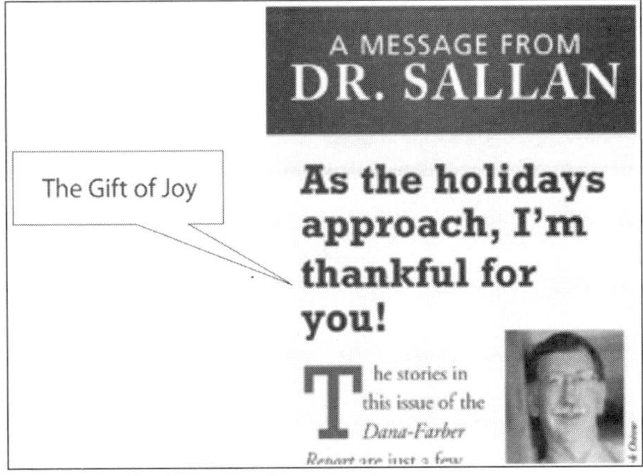

I've labeled each "Gift of Joy" in these four examples on this and facing page. Note that all appear in high-visibility locations such as headlines.

CHAPTER 31

Sad or happy? Both.

Which do you think will raise more money: a photo of a *sad* kid, a *neutral* kid or a *happy* kid?

If you said the sad photo, you're right.

Research from the American Marketing Association 2011 *Journal of Marketing Research*, reported by Jeff Brooks, found that a sad child photo raises 50% more than a photo of either a neutral or a happy child.

Sadness in a child touches the heart strings, right? Plus: if there are no problems to solve, donors have nothing to do.

So: *is* there any *lucrative* place for photos of *happy* kids . . . kids whose smiling, curious, intense, *unlined* faces SHOUT to the world that your under-sourced, difficult-to-execute, crazy-sounding programs are actually working for the next generation? And maybe after all there *is* reason to hope?

Yes. And we'll get to happy photos shortly. But first, let's understand what we're dealing with, psychologically.

Brain science helps you raise more money

Brains are organs. Those particular organs run our world and of course make all the gifts.

Since the human brain is so important to the survival of the planet and our species, countless scientists study it in ever-more-sophisticated ways.

And while there are many mysteries of the brain yet to be delved, some things we do now know to be true. For instance: there is a *biological* reason why unhappy images almost always raise more money.

It is a matter of stimulus/response. Built-in behavior. An unhappy image snags the mind's attention automatically, without your conscious thought or participation. Why? Because we are prey animals as well as hunters and alphas.

Welcome to what's in your head

We all have at the base of our skulls a lump of neurons popularly known as "the lizard brain." It's an early operating system, introduced at the start of the human evolutionary journey. (You might want to take a few seconds to touch that part of your head, just to say hello; maybe even thanks. It's sits about where your spinal cord enters the protective helmet of your skull.)

In the day, as we blinked primordial mud from our eyes, two alarming thoughts dominated our primitive processors. Both were survival messages:

1. "Can I eat it?"
2. "Will it kill me?"

Some things never change.

In modern skulls that early "lizard brain" has become what scientists call *the amygdala* (pronounced "ah-MIG-duh-la"; named for its almond-ish shape). The amygdala is still in charge much of the time. "Shown to play a key role in the processing of emotions, the amygdala [a lump of neurons] . . . is linked to both fear responses and pleasure," *Science Daily* says.[1]

The amygdala and its imperatives mean that anything distressing that enters my world (pictures of unhappy kids) gets more attention, faster, than anything safe and ignorable (pictures of smiling kids).

Negative and positive images: BOTH have their uses

As NYU neuroscientist Joseph LeDoux states in *Emotionomics*, "Negative emotions are linked to survival—and are much stronger."

I hope you smell as much opportunity as I do in Dr. LeDoux's statement. Still, you will encounter the yay-sayers. They don't believe in saying negative things—ever.

Steven Screen is a principal at Seattle-based The Better Fundraising Co. His clients range from WorldVision to Food For The Hungry to Mr. Holland's Opus Foundation.

Steven follows this simple guideline: use **negative** imagery in your appeals; use **positive** imagery in your thanks and newsletters.

Negative imagery drives giving.

Positive imagery reassures donors that something good has happened.

---

1 Here's a fun fact from *Science Daily:* "Its size is positively correlated with aggressive behavior across species. In humans, [the amygdala] . . . shrinks by more than 30% in males upon castration."

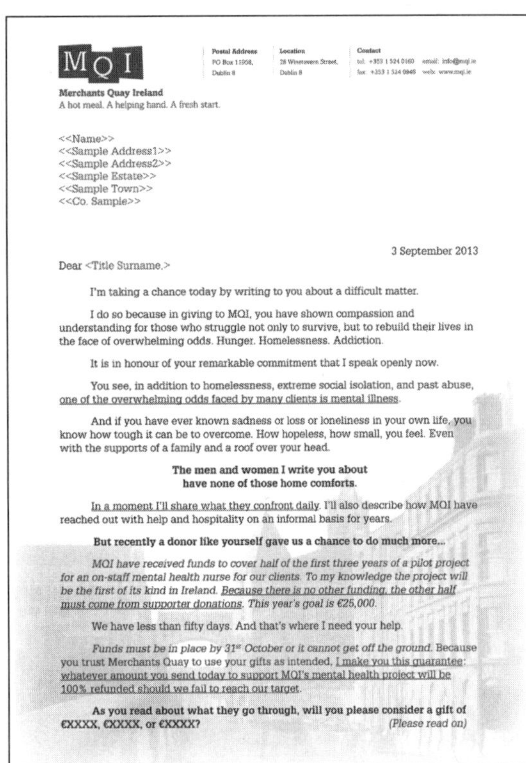

MQI

Postal Address
PO Box 11958,
Dublin 8

Location
28 Winetavern Street,
Dublin 8

Contact
tel: +353 1 524 0160 email: info@mqi.ie
fax: +353 1 524 0946 web: www.mqi.ie

Merchants Quay Ireland
A hot meal. A helping hand. A fresh start.

<<Name>>
<<Sample Address1>>
<<Sample Address2>>
<<Sample Estate>>
<<Sample Town>>
<<Co. Sample>>

3 September 2013

Dear <Title Surname.>

I'm taking a chance today by writing to you about a difficult matter.

I do so because in giving to MQI, you have shown compassion and understanding for those who struggle not only to survive, but to rebuild their lives in the face of overwhelming odds. Hunger. Homelessness. Addiction.

It is in honour of your remarkable commitment that I speak openly now.

You see, in addition to homelessness, extreme social isolation, and past abuse, one of the overwhelming odds faced by many clients is mental illness.

And if you have ever known sadness or loss or loneliness in your own life, you know how tough it can be to overcome. How hopeless, how small, you feel. Even with the supports of a family and a roof over your head.

The men and women I write you about have none of those home comforts.

In a moment I'll share what they confront daily. I'll also describe how MQI have reached out with help and hospitality on an informal basis for years.

But recently a donor like yourself gave us a chance to do much more...

MQI have received funds to cover half of the first three years of a pilot project for an on-staff mental health nurse for our clients. To my knowledge the project will be the first of its kind in Ireland. Because there is no other funding, the other half must come from supporter donations. This year's goal is €25,000.

We have less than fifty days. And that's where I need your help.

Funds must be in place by 31st October or it cannot get off the ground. Because you trust Merchants Quay to use your gifts as intended, I make you this guarantee: whatever amount you send today to support MQI's mental health project will be 100% refunded should we fail to reach our target.

As you read about what they go through, will you please consider a gift of €XXXX, €XXXX, or €XXXX? *(Please read on)*

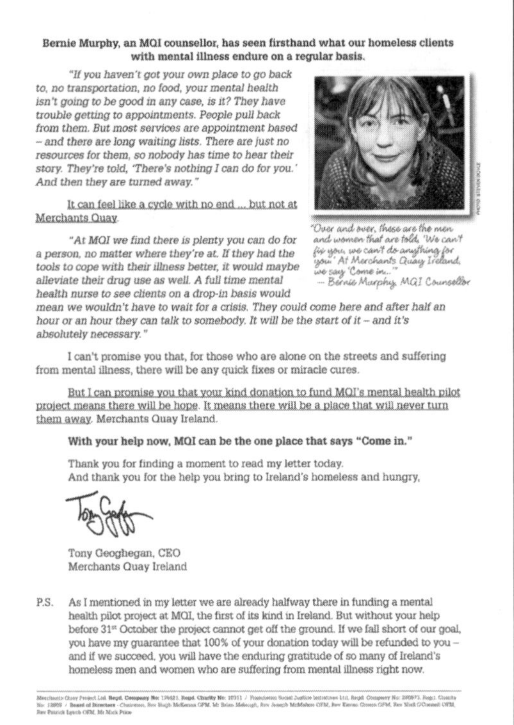

Bernie Murphy, an MQI counsellor, has seen firsthand what our homeless clients with mental illness endure on a regular basis.

"If you haven't got your own place to go back to, no transportation, no food, your mental health isn't going to be good in any case, is it? They have trouble getting to appointments. People pull back from them. But most services are appointment based – and there are long waiting lists. There are just no resources for them, so nobody has time to hear their story. They're told, 'There's nothing I can do for you.' And then they are turned away."

It can feel like a cycle with no end ... but not at Merchants Quay.

"Over and over, these are the men and women that are told, 'We can't fix you, we can't do anything for you.' At Merchants Quay Ireland, we say 'Come in...'"
— Bernie Murphy, MQI Counsellor

"At MQI we find there is plenty you can do for a person, no matter where they're at. If they had the tools to cope with their illness better, it would maybe alleviate their drug use as well. A full time mental health nurse to see clients on a drop-in basis would mean we wouldn't have to wait for a crisis. They could come here and after half an hour or an hour they can talk to somebody. It will be the start of it – and it's absolutely necessary."

I can't promise you that, for those who are alone on the streets and suffering from mental illness, there will be any quick fixes or miracle cures.

But I can promise you that your kind donation to fund MQI's mental health pilot project means there will be hope. It means there will be a place that will never turn them away. Merchants Quay Ireland.

With your help now, MQI can be the one place that says "Come in."

Thank you for finding a moment to read my letter today.
And thank you for the help you bring to Ireland's homeless and hungry,

Tony Geoghegan, CEO
Merchants Quay Ireland

P.S. As I mentioned in my letter we are already halfway there in funding a mental health pilot project at MQI, the first of its kind in Ireland. But without your help before 31st October the project cannot get off the ground. If we fall short of our goal, you have my guarantee that 100% of your donation today will be refunded to you – and if we succeed, you will have the enduring gratitude of so many of Ireland's homeless men and women who are suffering from mental illness right now.

As this letter's author, Lisa Sargent, wrote:

> This appeal from Merchants Quay Ireland to its active donors drew an enviable 21.21% response rate, with a handsome average gift of €109. In fewer than 14 days, it brought in €200,000.
>
> The impact? This one appeal fully funded a mental health nurse for Ireland's homeless for 3 full years, a pilot project that initially had no other source of funding. Three years later it's been such a successful program, the nurse position was just fully funded by the Irish government.
>
> MQI is, in 2017, expanding again . . . and again donors rallied to 100% fund two new positions. It's a wonderful, wonderful thing on a topic that most people won't touch with a ten foot pole because it's so shrouded in stigma, proving once again that donors are THE most amazing people on Earth—and proving how extraordinary MQI and their CEO Tony Geoghegan are in allowing the comms team to be open and honest, above all, with supporters.
>
> Key features (in addition to all the basics):
>
> - Money-back guarantee
> - Deadline
> - Matching challenge
> - No other source of funding available
> - Difficult issue, but a real, human, relatable one
>
> For the record: Yes, there was a *plan in place* to return anyone's donation who requested it. But to a person, what we got instead were phone calls, and notes tucked in with the donations, saying, "We really appreciate your offer to refund our money. Thank you so much for that. But please, even if you meet the goal, use what we've sent wherever it will do the most good for your clients who are hurting."
>
> In appeals, we use stock photos as stand-ins for clients, and fully disclose that to donors. They don't mind.
>
> Again, donors rock. Just saying.

Credits—Strategist: Denisa Casement, former head of fundraising, Merchants Quay Ireland; currently International Head of Individual Giving, Animals Asia. Copywriter: Lisa Sargent, Lisa Sargent Communications. Designer: Sandie Collette of S. Collette Design.

CHAPTER 32

What about "poverty porn"?

That close-up photo of a starving child with flies walking on his face? Critics call that "poverty porn." That haunting close-up of a little girl fleeing disaster? Poverty porn, again.

And yet, as science says, in fundraising appeals, sad pictures of kids raise FAR more money than pictures of neutral or happy kids. More important, evolution has made it so. Sadness stirs our souls . . . and, as a by-product, helps you meet your organization's fundraising goals.

Is there a middle ground?

Case study: How a photo changed a war's direction

How much did opposition to the Vietnam War stiffen in 1972 when . . .

. . . a picture of a screaming, skinny, 9-year-old girl splashed across the front pages of the global press?

a defining picture everyone of a certain age has seen and immediately recognizes today, more than 40 years later.

a picture of a small, terrified, naked child named Phan Thi Kim Phuc running toward us. A misplaced napalm strike on her village had ignited her clothing, and she'd torn it off.

back-peddling before that sudden rush, Nick Ut took his career-defining, Pulitzer Prize-winning shot.

In less than three years, under orders from Washington, the United States would finally quit the Vietnam War. Did one photo of a miserable child end the war? Not by itself, no. But it helped tell the story.

What you see in the field changes you

What's a fundraiser to do? What's the *right* thing to do? Show the sad picture? *Don't* show the sad picture and risk losing money?

Again: as Steven Screen notes, there's a right place for sad photos and a right place for happier photos. Think of them as "before and after" sets. The "before" photo shows the problem you're asking the donor to help solve. The "after" photo shows the good that can happen, with donor assistance.

I have never been in the field. I have seen sad things, yes. But I've never visited a refugee camp or a war zone or a village with only filthy, disease-bearing water to drink (as Scott Harrison did in West Africa, leading to his founding of charity: water).

I know that my annual income makes me richer than 98 percent of the other people on earth, according to CARE International. I know that, as an upper-middle-class American, I will make more money this year alone than a third of the world's population will make in a lifetime. What problems I have are first-world problems, the problems of privilege. I can't imagine what it really means to be truly poor.

Sad photos help with my lack of imagination, of course. But are they a distortion of the truth?

Can dignity and fundraising co-exist?

I asked a fundraiser who *has* been in the field to share her thoughts on why so many program staff distrust sad photos and label them poverty porn.

Gayle Gifford, ACFRE, co-founded Cause & Effect, a consulting firm, in 1996. Before that, she was director of development at PLAN USA. She is a longtime social activist and has authored several well-regarded books on boards. Here's Gayle's thoughtful reply:

> Here's an example that I believe captures the other side: Special Olympics.
>
> If you look at their images and copy, it's all upbeat. They serve athletes. Those athletes have courage, overcome obstacles, break through barriers, they are champions we root for.
>
> As far as I know, Special Olympics does not ever use photos or copy that imply that the kids it serves are pathetic. No one gets to call these kids "retarded" anymore or to see them as "other." They are our kids, and we celebrate in their victories.
>
> Do they do well in fundraising even so? According to GuideStar, over $88 million of Special Olympics' US revenue is philanthropy. And there are Special Olympics in just about every state and 170 countries.

It's this same attitude that is at the root of the concern about "poverty porn" Poor people around the world have dignity. They have "agency."

Poor people worldwide are incredibly resourceful to stay alive, raise kids, create small businesses (even if it is just selling little bags of water on the street as I saw kids do in Dakar), celebrate holidays and life events. Even in refugee camps, folks are trading, importing, finding firewood, etc.

What happens as copywriters is that when it's just about the pathetic kid and the "white messiah" as hero, we strip agency away from the people we are trying to raise money to help. And that infuriates many folks.

Another charge against us is that we get to do that because we are detached, they are foreign, we have privilege.

E.g., when did we get the release form from the parents of the malnourished child in Bangladesh whose photo we are showing so we could use the pathetic picture to raise money? They might very well say yes, but did we ask them? Did we even think we had to? We'd never consider it, using such a photo here in the States.

Now, am I saying "never"?

No, I'm not.

I think without photos we don't understand grinding poverty, death, the serious impact of war.

Are there terrible things happening and are the lives of the poor awful?

In many ways, yes . . . especially when they are dying of malnutrition, being raped in refugee camps, being slaughtered, etc. We want our photojournalists and reporters to show us these things so we can understand.

But like news media, when is that photo or story foremost about making money and selling papers (*if it bleeds it leads*) and when is it about changing hearts and minds. Creating common bonds, etc. What is our moral responsibility as fundraisers?

This is not an easy question . . . there is not one answer.

Maybe Ernie Schenck, award-winning advertising creative director, has the best last word on this peculiar topic.

In his Communications Arts column for May/June 2016, he wrote, "As any neuroscientist will tell you, the human brain is neuroplastic. That means it has a tendency to change the way it thinks according to ideas and attitudes that surround it. If those ideas and attitudes are positive, then the brain sees things through a positive lens. Subject it to a steady diet of negative stuff, and bingo—it suddenly starts seeing everything, and I mean everything, through a dark filter that can influence how you perceive your family, your friends, the people you work with. . . ."

You're selling hope. You're defeating despair. You need both hope and despair to fundraise. But they aren't created equal.

"Kids like Jenny need heroes like you." The envelope says it all. This kind of appeal has helped Barnardos (est. 1867 in London, after Dublin-born medical missionary Thomas Barnado saw homeless boys sleeping on roofs and in gutters) grow into a beloved, national charity helping the most vulnerable.

CHAPTER 33

Do you have an offer?

Jeff Brooks reckons that 40% of the gifts prompted by a direct mail appeal are due to the quality of your offer.

Another 40% of your success is due to the quality of the list: i.e., you mailed to the right people. The final 20%—the smallest bit—depends on the glory of your writing and design.

Putting the right offer in front of the right person at the right time: it is the classic, all-time secret of sales and marketing. By the way, in countries outside the Unuted States, the "offer" is also called the "proposition."

What is an offer?

An offer is an invitation to act, to say yes or no.

Every day, you weigh dozens of offers.

In a catalog you flip through, each item is an offer. When you buy lunch, "Would you like fries with that?" is an offer. When you visit a website, pretty much anything you can click on, including the word *more,* is in fact an offer.

Direct marketing professionals say, "The offer is king." By which they mean: *Find the right offer and response pours in.*

Conversely, without any offers, expect no response. I mention this because, for example, plenty of donor newsletters contain no offers at all. (And you wonder why no one ever calls or writes?)

What makes a good offer?

Steven Screen has this recipe:

- The problem is easy to understand.
- The solution is easy to understand.
- The cost is a good deal.
- There's urgency to solve the problem now.

The Fred Hollows Foundation, named for an Australian eye surgeon who pioneered inexpensive cataract operations in developing countries like Nepal, provides a perfect example of the Steven Screen offer:

> Many people stay needlessly blind because they live in poverty. In developing countries, blindness denies people education, independence and the ability to work—things which can break the poverty cycle. But all this can be changed with as little as $25.

Common offers

The most common offer is a variation on this plea: "Send us a gift. And with your help, we'll make the world a better place." Other frequent offers from fundraisers include:

- "For more information"
- An invitation to join an exclusive society such as a the Chancellor's Inner Circle
- An invitation to an event
- A free, informative brochure
- Free membership
- Discounted membership ("Your family membership entitles you to unlimited visits . . .")

- A member card
- A free subscription to your electronic or printed newsletter
- Special, timely updates from the president
- A free calendar of upcoming events and shows
- Discounts for advance purchase of tickets
- Special member-only previews
- Matching gift campaigns
- The ease and convenience of giving online
- A naming opportunity
- A behind-the-scenes tour
- A chance to volunteer
- Watch a video
- Advocate (send a letter to Congress)
- Tell your personal story
- Give us feedback, answer a survey
- A cow (see below)

Top 10 Reasons to Make a Commemorative Brick Gift to the Zoo

10. Celebrate a new birth
9. In memory of someone
8. Birthday gift
7. Retirement gift
6. Congratulations gift
5. Mother's Day gift
4. Father's Day gift
3. You love the Zoo
2. For the animals
1. To help make the Saint Louis Zoo the best zoo in the whole wide world

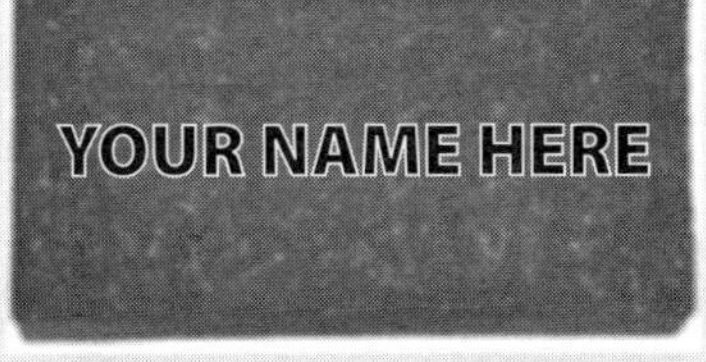

Heifer's four-footed offers: Making the intangible real

Heifer Project International (Little Rock, Arkansas; founded 1944; www.heifer.org) has a simple plan for ending world hunger: they give poor people livestock that produce food and income. They train people to keep these gift animals healthy and reproductive. It's the "teach a man to fish" philosophy in action.

Heifer calls their approach "the most important gift catalog in the world."

It offers donors the chance to buy an animal suitable for farming: a water buffalo, a llama, chickens, a flock of ducks, even honey bees. If you can't afford an entire pig this year ($120), you can buy a *share* of a pig for as little as $10. Heifer even has a gift registry, if you're looking "for a more meaningful way to celebrate events such as weddings, anniversaries, birthdays, graduations, and holidays."

There is an interesting communications strategy behind these offers. Heifer has taken something fairly intangible (its mission, and the donor's hope that "my gift will make the world a better place") and turned it into something *quite* tangible: a pig or other bountiful creature put into a person's needy hands. "Nothing's more satisfying than finding exactly the right solution to a problem," says Heifer. "That's the good feeling you get when you give an Asian subsistence farmer a water buffalo."

I can see it. Frankly, I can almost smell it.

Now in truth you are not buying a specific animal for a specific family in a specific country.

Heifer makes this clear in the fine print: "The prices in this catalog represent the complete livestock gift of a quality animal, technical assistance and training. Each purchase is symbolic and represents a contribution to the entire mission of Heifer International. Donations will be used where needed most to help struggling people."

So, yes, it's a symbolic purchase. But the bottom line is, somebody somewhere still gets a cow.

The communications lesson is this: when you can make your mission more tangible, it's easier for the prospect to imagine the result. In turn, when prospects can easily imagine the result, they're more likely to become donors. They can SEE the mission in their mind's eye. It's real. It's not a promise. It's a promise *fulfilled.*

Heifer International has made its mission tangible through livestock offers. What can *you* offer that will tangibly symbolize your mission? A university selling $2 million endowed chairs offers pictures of 20 assorted chairs, different styles from different periods, throne to recliner, wittily chosen. Each has a space on it labeled, "Your name here."

Don't bury your offer

Placing your offer ("Call this number for more information") at the end of a long article **guarantees that most people will miss it**. It will be skimmed as just another chunk of prose in an article they probably didn't read in the first place (as eye-motion studies reveal).

The solution: celebrate every offer you make.

Turn it into a LOUD advertisement.

Make your offer BIG, **bold**, easy to spot.

Opera Ball 2011: My Fair Ladies...

WOULDN'T IT BE LOVERLY (TO RAISE A MILLION DOLLARS)?

Mark your calendars for **April 9, 2011**...Rudy Avelar, HGO's "dean of patron services," is chairing this season's Opera Ball! As you'd expect, Rudy's special touch promises to make "My Fair Ladies" a truly glorious evening.

A favorite part of the Ball is the annual silent auction, co-chaired this year by Anna Dean and Wade Wilson. It will feature a wide-ranging collection of luxury items: jewelry, clothing, vacations, spa services, artworks, and more. Proceeds benefit Houston Grand Opera and all its extraordinary programs.

Here are just a few ways that you can enhance this auction:

- Donate a bottle of your favorite wine.
- Underwrite dinner for four at a restaurant you love
- Sponsor a spree at a special store you know your fellow opera lovers would enjoy
- Offer tickets to an upcoming concert – show off Houston's magnificent performing arts scene!

You can dance all night...and you can help make Rudy's Opera Ball even more special. **To purchase tickets or to donate to the silent auction, please call Guyla Pircher at 713-546-0277.**

Rudy Avelar, this season's Opera Ball Chair.

Rudy invites *you* to make Opera Ball 2011 unforgettable

Mark your calendars for **April 9, 2011**...Rudy Avelar, HGO's "prince of patron services," is chairing this season's Opera Ball! As you'd expect, Rudy's special touch promises to make "My Fair Ladies" a truly glorious evening.

A favorite part of the Ball is the annual silent auction, co-chaired this year by Anna Dean and Wade Wilson. It will feature a wide-ranging collection of luxury items: jewelry, clothing, vacations, spa services, artworks, and more. Proceeds benefit Houston Grand Opera and all its extraordinary programs.

Here are just a few ways that you can enhance this auction:

- Donate a bottle of your favorite wine.
- Underwrite dinner for four at a restaurant you love
- Sponsor a spree at a special store you know your fellow opera lovers would enjoy
- Offer tickets to an upcoming concert – show off Houston's magnificent performing arts scene!

You can dance all night...and help make Rudy's Opera Ball even more special. **To purchase tickets or to donate to the silent auction, please call Guyla Pircher at 713-546-0277.**

Rudy Avelar, this season's Opera Ball Chair.

On the left, the Houston Grand Opera buries its offer. On the right, the HGO unearths its offer by swapping a clever headline for a clear headline and putting the offer itself into a box like a small ad.

Happy Mother's Day!

I made a gift to Central Berkshire Habitat for Humanity in honor of you, the amazing woman in my life.

The Central Berkshire (MA) Habitat for Humanity offered donors a special way to celebrate Mother's Day, with a gift in honor of . . .

"Insider" tours are a great way to make lifelong friends, friends who will never stop talking about what they experienced personally. The "Hidden Zoo Tour" offer was built into the capital campaign booklet for Roger Williams Park Zoo (Providence, RI). Creative: Northeast Design.

CHAPTER 34

Grade level

Grade level is a horribly misleading technical term.

The term suggests, to non-professionals, that writing at the 4th-grade level is suited only for 4th-graders, whereas writing at the 12th-grade level is suited for those who have graduated high school.

Wrong. Totally.

Grade level, as scored by standard scales, has nothing to do with a reader's level of educational attainment.

In donor communications, grade level measures just one thing: *How fast can the reader's brain absorb your prose?*

Consider these two readability reports, generated by Microsoft Word. First, please notice the "averages." Second, notice the "readability" scores, both Flesch Reading Ease and Flesch-Kincaid Grade.

Readability Statistics	
Counts	
Words	479
Characters	2258
Paragraphs	32
Sentences	40
Averages	
Sentences per Paragraph	1.4
Words per Sentence	11.4
Characters per Word	4.5
Readability	
Passive Sentences	0%
Flesch Reading Ease	67.4
Flesch-Kincaid Grade Level	6.6
OK	

Readability Statistics	
Counts	
Words	1259
Characters	7129
Paragraphs	19
Sentences	49
Averages	
Sentences per Paragraph	3.1
Words per Sentence	24.8
Characters per Word	5.5
Readability	
Passive Sentences	12%
Flesch Reading Ease	28.7
Flesch-Kincaid Grade Level	12.0
OK	

The numbers in the readability report *on the left* score a direct mail acquisition appeal that broke records for a Planned Parenthood affiliate.

The numbers in the readability report *on the right* score a committee-written case for a capital campaign, from one of the smartest universities on earth, filled to the rafters with Nobel Laureates.

Focus on just two measures: Flesch Reading Ease and Flesch-Kincaid Grade Level.

The highly successful direct mail on the left: Ease: 67. Level: 7. Science says this direct mail will be a brisk read for everyone.

The committee-written insider case for support on the right: Ease: 29. Level: 12 (which is as high as the scoring goes on my computer). Science says this thick prose will be a slog for every reader . . . even a Ph.D.

Your executive director and some board members may protest: *I don't believe it.* They suffer from ignorance. It should be the fundraiser's decision.

Your donor communications can bring ease and clarity (a good customer service experience). Or your donor communications can bring extra mental labor (a lousy customer service experience). Which of these two will your donors appreciate most?

"Sounds like conversation." Some will object . . .

Of course, if you admit that you're writing intentionally at the 7th-grade level, someone will sniff with disdain. "We're an engineering school, for goodness sake," the typical argument goes. "Most of our donors have graduate degrees. We can't *risk* talking down to them."

Sounds logical. But that presumption is wrong.

In the world of donor communications, there is no place for obfuscation and erudition. Save that for academic journals. Writing at a lower grade level is not at all about talking *down*. It's about talking *clearly* and communicating *quickly*.

A professional copywriter can write about the discoveries of 21st-century astrophysics at the 8th-grade level. (And if you're writing for a general audience, one *should* write at that grade level or lower.)

Grade level and reading ease scores have little to do with the scope of your vocabulary. After all, a computer running a formula decides your grade level and reading ease scores. That computer is not reading your prose in any human sense. It doesn't understand you. That computer is simply counting. It's counting words, syllables, spaces. It's calculating ratios of long to short. It rewards short words, short sentences, short paragraphs.

If most of your sentences are simply constructed, if you keep multisyllabic words to a minimum, if your paragraphs are not deep and dense, you'll do fine.

Reality check

The preceding 5-paragraph passage scores at the 7th-grade level, by the way. *Did it seem like I was talking down to you?*

Pennsylvania and many other states now require that insurance policies score no higher than the 9th-grade level on Flesch-Kincaid. Novels written for airport book stores score at the 4th-grade level. And *The Wall Street Journal* hovers around the 9th-grade level, reporting on everything under the sun.

And where did Flesch-Kincaid scoring originate, you wonder? With the US Navy. The Navy needed technical manuals for F-15s that someone with a high school education could understand. They contracted with J. Peter Kincaid, a psychologist and university professor, and the Flesch-Kincaid grading system was born. Soon after, it became the Department of Defense's military standard for all technical manuals.

Kincaid verified and applied the methods and insights of Dr. Rudolf Flesch (1911–1986). Flesch, a Viennese lawyer who fled the Nazis and resettled in New York, published many books on the subject of clear, effective communication. *TIME* magazine dubbed him the "Mr. Fix-It of writing." He was also known as "the man who taught Associated Press how to write." I have his 1949 book, *The Art of Readable Writing*, a gift from Steve Herlich. But Flesch's most famous book became *Why Johnny Can't Read: And What You Can Do about It*. That book inspired Dr. Seuss to write *The Cat in the Hat*.

The preceding paragraph scores at the 8th-grade level. Did it seem like I was talking down to you?

Final word goes to the late, great George Smith (1940–2012), writer for Oxfam, Amnesty, Greenpeace, Unicef, WWF and many more. He said, "All fundraising copy should sound like someone talking."[1]

It *should* sound like conversation, not oration.

If you're looking for a pomposity-detector, grade-level scores are the measures of choice.

1 George Smith, *Tiny Essentials of Writing for Fundraising* ([city of publication]: White Lion Press, 2003).

CHAPTER 35

First things first: "Anchoring"

Be careful what you say first.

It can help you. Or it can just as easily hurt you, money-wise.

In 2015, Leah Eustace, "principal and Chief Idea Goddess" at Good Works, one of Canada's best fundraising agencies, shared Nobel Prize-winning psychologist Daniel Kahneman's eye-opening experiments on "anchoring" and giving with the Nonprofit Storytelling Conference.[1]

The featured campaign aimed to save 50,000 sea birds. Dr. Kahneman tested three different types of asks.

- "Would you be willing to pay $5 . . . ?"
- "What would you be willing to pay?"
- "Would you be willing to pay $400 . . . ?

As you'll note, the first ask **started** with a very, very small amount . . . something even a college kid could afford, bypassing a latte.

The second ask was open-ended. In effect, it said: "Dear Donor, You decide what saving those birds is worth, knowing your bank account and your personal values."

The third ask **started** with a large amount. Not *improbably* large . . . but large enough to get the attention of 99% of the population.[2]

Dr. Kahneman's test results will teach you everything you need to know, practically speaking, about why anchoring can be so useful.

The first ask in his experiment brought in an average gift of just $20.

The second open-ended ask brought in an average gift of $64.

The third ask, beginning with a large number, brought in an average gift of $143.

---

1 As reported by Mark Neigh, November 15, 2015, in the Masterworks blog.

2 You might not think that $400 is all that much, particularly if you're affluent; you've seen too many dinner tabs. Fact is, the vast majority of US households make very few charitable gifts of $400 and above in one lump sum. They aren't cheapskates: each gives away something like $3,000 a year. But that total is spread across up to 20 charities. Single $400 gifts are rare.

"Anchoring" expanded

Anchoring could be summed up this way: *Whatever information we encounter first will set up our expectations.*

As brain evolution goes, is this one of humanity's better adaptations? Who knows: it's there. We have a "cognitive bias." It is "the common human tendency to rely too heavily on the first piece of information offered (the 'anchor') when making decisions. For example, the initial price offered for a used car sets the standard for the rest of the negotiations, so that prices lower than the initial price seem more reasonable even if they are still higher than what the car is really worth."[3]

As Dr. Kahneman's test showed, when your suggested first gift is a mere $5, you push the donor's expectations down, toward the low end. A low first number brought in a low average gift. A high first number brought in a high average gift.

But anchoring theory doesn't just apply to numbers. As Leah elaborated, "That first piece of information—first photo, first character, first word, first number, first emotion, first impression—is critically important."

Avoiding the third dot

Anchoring is about putting first things first. Anchoring is about rewarding your true believers by giving them the lead position in your parade, not at the tail, as an also-ran.

Let's examine this statement:

> "Bella came to us as a very sick kitty. But we gave her the healing help she needed, thanks to your gifts."

Sounds normal, right? Reasonable? Garden variety? Polite? Pretty much what you *should* say?

Consider, though, the *order* in which you said things: first comes the sick kitty, *then* the charity's work, *then* the donor's gifts.

The sick kitty anchors the statement. The next most important part is the organization's work. Last in line is the donor, almost as an afterthought.

Of course, you don't *mean* it to sound like an afterthought; you're trying to give credit where credit's due. But you're not taking advantage of anchoring, either.

As a general way of speaking, to build a thriving culture of philanthropy, there are two dots you want to connect as directly as you can:

3 Wikipedia.

- Dot #1: the act of giving
- Dot #2: the good that can happen, thanks to that act of giving

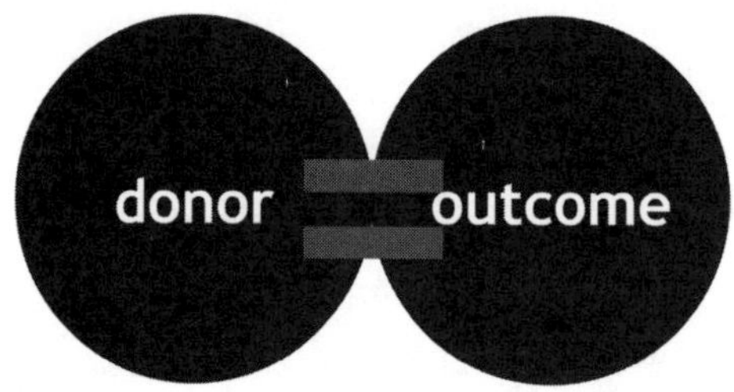

Often, though, the charity inserts a third dot in the middle: *itself*. As in: "Bella came to us as a very sick kitty. But we gave her the healing help she needed, thanks to your gifts."

That dot in the middle is a problem. It casts a big shadow. And who's demoted? The donor.

Here's a rewrite of the same statement, this time consciously taking advantage of anchoring and humankind's cognitive bias:

> "Thanks to your gifts, Bella is no longer a very sick kitty. Thanks to your gifts, Bella got the healing help she needed . . . just in time. You're her hero!"

CHAPTER 36

What's your SMIT?

SMIT is an acronym.

It stands (incompletely) for "Single Most Important Thing (SMIT) I have to tell you today." I first learned about the SMIT concept from Jonathon Grapsas. I'm told he learned SMIT from Pareto, Australia's biggest commercial direct mail and fundraising agency, his employer at the time. And so key ideas spread.

I decide on my SMIT before I write anything to a donor. And I keep it simple, as in: "We have a matching gift offer to promote. Focus on that." Here's a successful direct mail appeal based on exactly that SMIT.

> Dear Tom,
>
> I have a favor to ask you . . . an *important* favor.
>
> Here's what has happened. It's very good news.
>
> A Bishop Ward alumnus in a nearby state has put a donation of $250,000 on the table.
>
> But there's a condition, before we can claim that quarter-million dollars in new financial support: **other donors have to help match his gift**, one for one.
>
> To claim his entire gift of $250,000 . . . so we can put it *all* to work in our classrooms, for our young scholars . . . I need your help with the match. With your help, Bishop Ward will gain in total a half million dollars in support. That kind of money can have a huge impact.
>
> If you give to no other appeal this year, please consider giving to this once-in-a-blue-moon matching-gift opportunity. I've enclosed an envelope for your convenience. Or you can instantly make your matching gift online, at *www.wardhigh.org.*
>
> When you give this time, you'll get *twice* the "bang for your buck." Your $10 gift will expand to $20 of impact. Your $500 gift will balloon to become a massive $1,000 of impact.

Please . . . help Bishop Ward make this vital goal.

Notice how the letter returns over and over to the matching gift offer. The SMIT never quits. It's also highlighted on the reply device:

> Absolutely, Father Michael!
>
> Let's claim *every penny* of that $250,000 match. My matching gift for the students of Bishop Ward High School is enclosed.

You know those "invisible fences" used to train dogs to stay inside their own yard? The company buries a wire antenna around the perimeter of your property. If your dog tries to step past that perimeter, the antenna signals the dog's electronic collar and administers a small shock called a "correction."

Think of your SMIT that way. Whenever you're tempted to wander off, give yourself a SMIT correction and re-focus.

CHAPTER 37

Mental nods

In his Munich laboratory, Dr. Siegfried Vögele, author of the influential *Handbook of Direct Mail*, videotaped people as they read through commercial sales letters.

In those videos, he observed an important phenomenon: sometimes people physically nodded, if they agreed with something they'd just read.

That led him to postulate the idea of "mental nods." Recipients of your digital and print appeals don't have to *visibly* nod as they read. But they *do* have to agree with you: mentally nod along. The more mental nods you get, the more likely someone in the end will decide to make a gift.

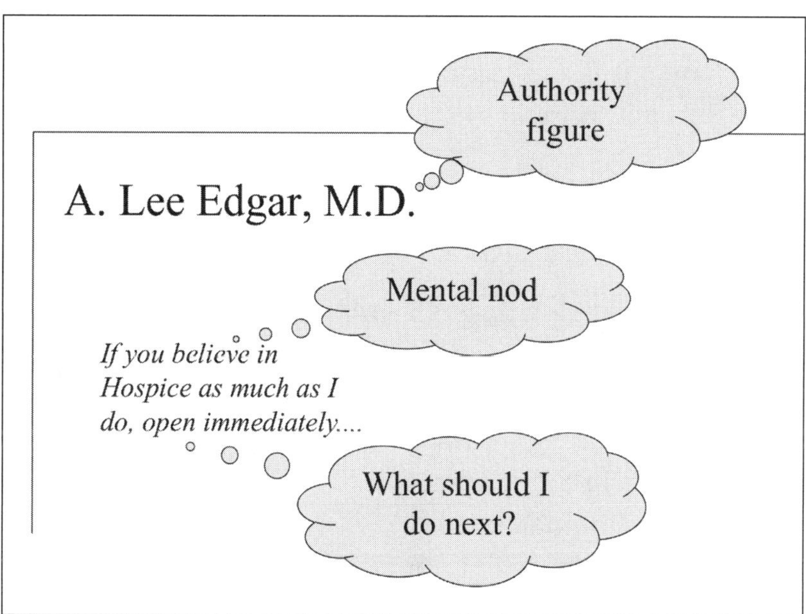

This is the outbound envelope for an effective hospice "conversion" direct mail appeal. It was sent for about a decade to anyone who had made a gift to a certain hospice "in lieu of flowers," as the family requested. The hope was to convert some of these "in lieu of" donors into annual donors. This letter performed well in that task. I've labeled with balloons a few things. We used an MD whose own wife died in hospice care as the letter's signer; that gave us an "authority" trigger, following the research of Robert Cialdini. Then we included a "mental nod" statement ("If you believe . . .") to separate quickly the interested from the disinterested. Then we told people what action to take next (". . . open immediately . . ."). That last thing is basic direct mail theory and practice: NEVER leave it to people to figure out; ALWAYS tell them what to do next.

CHAPTER 38

The perfect length for a direct mail appeal

At the end of 2016, in a professional Facebook group, a new and bewildered fundraiser raised this oft-discussed issue: *How long* should *an appeal letter be?*

She'd written a one-page appeal and sent it to her board for review. The board had added a kitchen sink or two . . . and now the letter was up to four pages. She wondered: was four pages OK?

More than two dozen other fundraisers soon chimed in with their comments. On the issue of page count:

- "In my opinion, less is more. People see too much text and don't read."
- "I agree. The longer it is, the less likely people are to read all of it. I think you were right to do a one-pager."
- "Yeah, I agree: 4 pages is probably too long. People won't read all that."
- "4 page appeal letter? No way."
- "There's no way I'd ever slog through a four-page appeal letter, much less send a donation after receiving it."

Again, these are fundraisers, capable professionals supposedly, or at least eager-to-get-it-right beginners in the fundraising field. Yet their comments reveal zero knowledge of direct mail fundamentals.

And it's not like direct mail is a minor factor in fundraising. As industry expert Mal Warwick has noted, "Fundraising letters are—by far—the single biggest means used by nonprofits to recruit new donors."[1]

The dismissive comment said with full conviction ("There's no way . . .") is the most dangerous. It suggests that four-page letters actually *kill* response. (Wrong.) It suggests that every four-page letter is a slog. (Wrong.) And if someone in power—your boss or board chair—had said that very same thing to you, you'd probably acquiesce. "Yeah, I guess you're right. Four-page letters are a bad idea."

---

1 Blog posted March 7, 2013, on Mal Warwick | Donordigital.

Thus the great wheel of nonprofit ignorance unprofitably grinds on, driven by opinions, not knowledge.

Page count was never the point; training is

I know: it's counterintuitive. But here's the thing . . .

While a LOUSY four-page letter will *not* outperform a LOUSY one-page letter, a GREAT four-page letter *will* outperform a GREAT one-page letter, 19 times out of 20.

Why? *Because page count doesn't really matter.*

Is the offer clear and repeated? Is the donor-centricity heavy and heartfelt? Is the letter conversational? Is it skimmable? Is there a page-turner story to draw the reader in?

The ignorant will assume and surmise and disagree about page length. But it's a false concern.

Among top direct mail professionals worldwide, there is zero debate: they expect to get their strongest results writing longer letters . . . and they test that assumption a lot. "Long letters pretty much always do better [in those tests]," Jeff Brooks told me. "And that's true for acquisition as well as donor cultivation."

And why wouldn't they? Professionally written letters work hard to entertain you, to grab you, to keep you on the edge of your seat, to draw you in and onward. Masterful letters are fast, built for skimming. They're warm and flattering. They tell a vivid story of urgent need . . . and treat you, the donor, as a hero.

If you can't afford an agency

Most charities can't afford high-performing direct mail agencies like Pareto (Australia); Bluefrog (UK); Ask Direct (Ireland); Agents of Good, Stephen Thomas, Good Works, Harvey McKinnon (all Canadian); or TrueSense (US).

Most charities go with letters written in-house. With those letters, shorter is better.

Make your ask, be grateful, be polite, be brief and be gone.

One of the most successful appeal letters I know was written by a volunteer for a small-town library. After attending two brief workshops, she wrote a one-page letter that raised almost $60,000 from 4,600 households.

After attending two workshops.

To succeed consistently with direct mail, you *must* get training. It doesn't have to be a lot of training. But it has to be something; maybe just a visit to sofii.org, where for free you have full access to Jerry Huntsinger's direct mail tutorials.

You cannot *guess* your way to success in direct-mail fundraising. For one thing, effective direct mail has a lot of behind-the-scenes machinery you should know your way around. One reason four-page letters do better? There's plenty of room to accommodate that complicated machinery without resorting to 10-point type.

At a minimum, read the frequently updated classic, Mal Warwick's *How to Write Successful Fundraising Appeals*. The latest edition (2013) covers both postal and emailed appeals.

And for good measure, and an even deeper understanding of the writer's thought process, get a copy of Jeff Brooks' *The Fundraiser's Guide to Irresistible Communications* or his latest, *How to Turn Your Words into Money*.

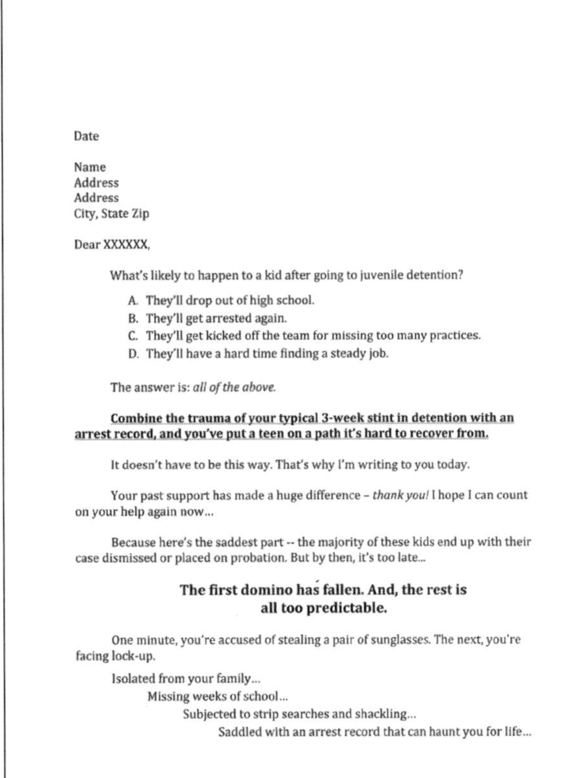

Date

Name
Address
Address
City, State Zip

Dear XXXXXX,

What's likely to happen to a kid after going to juvenile detention?

A. They'll drop out of high school.
B. They'll get arrested again.
C. They'll get kicked off the team for missing too many practices.
D. They'll have a hard time finding a steady job.

The answer is: *all of the above.*

Combine the trauma of your typical 3-week stint in detention with an arrest record, and you've put a teen on a path it's hard to recover from.

It doesn't have to be this way. That's why I'm writing to you today.

Your past support has made a huge difference – *thank you!* I hope I can count on your help again now...

Because here's the saddest part -- the majority of these kids end up with their case dismissed or placed on probation. But by then, it's too late...

The first domino has fallen. And, the rest is all too predictable.

One minute, you're accused of stealing a pair of sunglasses. The next, you're facing lock-up.

Isolated from your family...
Missing weeks of school...
Subjected to strip searches and shackling...
Saddled with an arrest record that can haunt you for life...

It doesn't matter if your case is dismissed... or, if you're found innocent....

Your future has changed forever. That's how the system works.

And that's why I need your help.

Because you have the power to change all this...

Barbed wire at this juvenile detention center isn't the only similarity to adult prisons. Kids are also subjected to strip searches when they arrive and after seeing visitors – some refuse to see their parents or family to avoid this violation.

You have the power to turn handcuffs into high school diplomas for kids across Massachusetts.

Juvenile detention is traumatic.

Kids are handcuffed, shackled, and strip searched.

They live in **jail-like conditions, sleeping in locked rooms with strangers** who might be much bigger and much older than they are.

Many kids will even refuse visitors, including their parents, because they have to endure a strip search after each and every visit.

You and I both know there are less destructive and less costly ways to hold youth accountable...

Study after study proves -- incarcerating teenagers sets them up to be high school dropouts, unable to find a job, and more likely to commit future crimes.

That's why Citizens for Juvenile Justice supports alternatives to court processing to hold kids accountable while also getting them what they need...

At the heart of diversion is a belief I know you and I both share... it's the belief that locking kids up should only be used as a last resort.

That's why Citizens for Juvenile Justice is promoting a law that would allow courts to **direct kids to more appropriate programs, treatment, or community service before they are arraigned or sent to detention.**

A masterly four-page renewal appeal letter written by Tina Cincotti with design by Wendy Brovold. The letter achieved a strong 22% response rate, with an increase in average gift amount of 24%.

It's a game changer for the future of so many kids.

Here's what you make possible when you support alternative ways to hold kids accountable...

- Time spent in the classroom, not the courtroom
- Time spent at sports, counseling, or in extracurricular activities, instead of at a youth detention center
- No interruption of special education or mental health services
- No removal from the home or isolation from family and friends
- Freedom to pursue education and employment without the lifelong burden of a criminal record

You can make all of this a reality for kids across the Commonwealth by lending your support again today.

Diverting low-level cases from court isn't just morally right, it's also less expensive than lock-up.

Diversion programs cost $60-150 a day versus $300 a day for detention. Not to mention the cost of the lost future of each kid in lock-up...

In areas of the state with diversion programs in place, the results speak for themselves. One example is the City of Cambridge where police have established a diversion program for first-time offenders. Juvenile arrests are down 57% since the program began.

But, not everyone has equal access to diversion programs.

It all depends on where you live...

Some counties offer non-court options for kids who run into trouble, including restorative justice programs in many suburban towns.

Other counties, including Suffolk County, with large, low-income communities of color, have no formal pre-arraignment diversion program.

Kids in detention sleep on "beds" like these in a locked room with strangers. Younger children with minor infractions can end up near older kids with more serious charges.

Almost no county tracks outcomes for the kids they divert, and they don't keep track of whether they are offering these chances to all kids equally.

You can help make diversion an option that is offered fairly to kids in all counties by donating to Citizens for Juvenile Justice today.

Here at Citizens for Juvenile Justice, we are working day and night advocating for legislation and other reforms that would make evidence-driven, diversion programs available across Massachusetts.

> *"Rather than providing a public safety benefit, processing a juvenile through the system appears to have a negative or backfire effect. This was especially true [when compared] with a diversion program."*
> ~ Research Review by the U.S. Department of Justice

But we're running out of time... The Legislature adjourns in July!

I hope I can count on your support now to raise the money needed to push this bill across the finish line before July 31st.

This legislation would mean fewer kids charged and incarcerated, more consistency across counties and courtrooms, and safer communities for us all.

With your generous support again today, we can pass this legislation and put the "justice" in the juvenile justice system.

Together, we can create a better future for all our kids.

Thank you so much for considering this request!

Most sincerely,

Naoka Carey
Executive Director

P.S. If you believe classrooms are a better place for children than courtrooms, I hope you'll send a gift now! **With the legislative session ending in July, time is running out to ensure that children in Massachusetts have appropriate alternatives to court and lock-up.** Please respond today! Together, we can create brighter futures for kids and safer communities for us all. Thank you for your continued support!

CHAPTER 39

One-line opening paragraphs

The surest way to stop a potential reader from going any deeper is to insist she bushwhack a path through your dense opening paragraph . . . whether it's in a direct mail appeal, an emailed newsletter, the chair's letter in the annual report, or your "Who We Are" statement on the website.

A single vibrant sentence—a single, very short paragraph surrounded by white space—is far, far, far more effective at igniting interest in a reader with a cold brain.

Something like this.

Something so simple and clean it penetrates without any extra effort my rapidly skimming and not-especially-alert brain.

Consider these teensy openings from four successful direct mail appeals. Note how pedestrian they are:

This Memorial Day, you and I will share something special . . .

Will you join this important celebration?

You can hear the wicked glee in their voices.

Welcome . . . I hope.

Direct mail wunderkind Joseph Sugarman, in his frank and brilliant book, *Advertising Secrets of the Written Word*,[1] makes an important point.

"If the reader doesn't read your very first sentence, chances are that he or she won't read your second sentence." And hence won't make a purchase . . . or, in the case of fundraising, a gift.

1 Joseph Sugarman, *Advertising Secrets of the Written Word* (Las Vegas: DelStar Books, 1998): 31.

"Now if the first sentence is so important," Sugarman says, "what can you do to make it so compelling to read, so simple, and so interesting that your readers—every one of them—will read it in its entirety? The answer: Make it short."

And yet they will say "Nay!"

Expect resistance from the untrained, of course.

Simone Joyaux watched a fundraiser proudly hand her proposed new direct mail appeal to a board member, hoping for approval.

The appeal began with a one-word paragraph: "Help. . . ."

The board member handed the letter back hastily, lips curled down. "Is this how we plan to represent our organization," she said with dripping disdain, "as the 'grammatically incorrect' organization?"

Was this board member right to worry?

Absolutely not.

She had applied rules from some incongruous world she knew well—a grammar class of the 1960s, maybe?—to a world she didn't know at all: fundraising through the mail.

Her objection was well-intentioned, of course. It just wasn't relevant.

Her objection was based on ignorance, uttered unfortunately from a position of power.

Gravity is a force to be reckoned with, if you're attempting space travel. Board ignorance is a force to be reckoned with, if you're attempting fundraising.

Breaking the silence

Here are some sample direct mail appeal openings written by a professional copywriter. Feel free to steal and adapt.

> Dear Jane Sample,
>
> The doctors call it "Day Zero."
>
> It's the day you come back from the dead.
>
> ------
>
> Dear Ms. Sample,
>
> Let me ask you a personal question: Do you believe in miracles?
>
> ------

Dear Mr. Sample,

Healing . . .a strong family . . . stable communities . . . and a place in this world for every child.

Dear Mr. Sample,

"If I sell enough lemonade I can pay for the broken window that made Dad leave Mom."

"My mom has Ades. She is very sick in bed. She dies. I am sad. I dies and I see her in heven. Then I am happy."

"This is my baby sister after she fell down the stairs. My Mom says she falls down the stairs a lot."

You think: there's no hope.

But there is hope. And there is healing . . . every day . . . for even the most difficult childhood emotional problems. When you give a gift to Bradley Hospital.

Dear Ms. Sample,

Here's my promise to you.

Dear Mr. Sample,

Soon it will be tax time again. Perhaps not the happiest thought, but there could be a silver lining . . . if you make a gift to Bryant now.

Dear Ms. Sample,

A few days from now a Bryant representative will call you, asking you to renew and, if possible, increase your gift to the College.

I'm writing you in advance—parent to parent—to explain why I think it's important that you say "Yes" when that phone call comes.

Dear John Sample,

Lisa and I are writing today to bare our souls: Island Arts needs your help.

Dear Jessica Sample,

I'm writing you today to ask that you consider making a gift.

And you're probably wondering, "Why?"

Here's my answer . . .

Because your gift to [NGO] has the power to solve some of America's thorniest community development problems. Your gift says "Yes!" when so many others would say, "No, it's impossible."

CHAPTER 40

To P.S.? Or not to P.S.?

Professor Siegfried Vögele: "Over 90 percent of readers read the 'PS' before the letter. It is the first paragraph, not the last."[1]

This discovery means your PS can be one of the hardest-working elements in your appeal letter. It's a high-visibility place where you can make a great first impression . . . or, of course, not.

Professor Vögele (1931–2014) employed cameras in his pioneering research. He watched how people normally interact with direct mail.

He observed them conduct what he called an "initial run-through . . . a self-orientation." In these first few seconds readers were asking, "'What is this then?' 'What does it mean?' 'What do they want from me?' 'Do I need it?' 'Should I read it?' etc."

He also noted, "Only the person who has dictated or written the letter himself begins right at the top and reads slowly down to the signature, line by line. He [is] checking and looking for any possible errors."

The recipient, on the other hand, leaps instantly to the end. "[When] a . . . letter has a signature, the eyes rush down to this signature first of all and only then . . . is [the recipient] subconsciously ready to read the letter right from the top."

Direct mail is a physical interaction with the recipient's eyes and touch. Because it's physical, automatically the emotions are engaged. The brain begins its hunt immediately. It seeks novelty foremost. Biology demands one thing: sort the world as fast as possible into new (i.e., possibly dangerous, in our remote evolutionary past) and safe.

It's a free-range brain, too: it leaps from place to place.

To the salutation first: "Are they talking to me?"

To the signature next (and nothing in between *except maybe* that tiny opening sentence you've crafted): "Who signed this?"

So, yeah, try to be new and different when you can.

What does an effective P.S. look like?

Copywriting superstar Mal Warwick admonishes: "[Don't] use the postscript to restate and reinforce the ask. The overwhelming majority of fundraising letters

1 Siegfried Vögele, *Handbook of Direct Mail* (New York: Prentice Hall, 1992): 202.

make that mistake. Simply pleading with the reader to 'act now' or 'send your gift today' is a waste of this valuable real estate. That's boring. Use the P.S. instead to disclose some benefit or intriguing fact . . . . Make the P.S. irresistibly interesting."[2]

Yes and no.

Mal was one of the most accomplished direct mail people on the planet. The most useful book I've ever encountered, in terms of "lucrative ideas per page," is his *How to Write Successful Fundraising Appeals* (regularly updated).

Yet I've succeeded with direct mail appeals where the PS really does nothing more than repeat the essential offer.

Don't overthink this, is my basic advice. Here are three postscripts from appeals I wrote that did very well. The first simply repeats the letter's SMIT (Single Most Important Thing I have to share with you today): a matching gift offer.

> P.S. Double your impact . . . if you join today!

The three-paragraph postscript from a different letter also repeats the SMIT: please join our family of true believers. Then doubles down on the thanks.

> PS: I know many other worthy causes plead for your help each year. Please know how honored PPMNS will be if you choose today to join our supporter family!
>
> Thank you.
>
> I can't tell you that enough.

And finally, here's another SMIT-driven postscript, this time for a community hospital that offers satisfied patients the chance to honor a physician or other caregiver through its Guardian Angel program.

> P.S. Hearing the words "thank you" from a patient means more to a caregiver than any prestigious accolade or award he or she can receive.
>
> Now you can acknowledge a doctor, nurse, or other caregiver through Sharp HealthCare Foundation's Guardian Angel program. It will be a special way to honor someone who has touched your life in an important way.
>
> I hope you'll read the enclosed note from Katy Green, R.N., Guardian Angel recipient.

If you find yourself underwhelmed by my creative genius, good. If you think, "I could have written any of those!" you're absolutely right. You can do this.

---

2 Mal Warwick, *How to Write Successful Fundraising Appeal* (San Francisco: Jossey-Bass): 92.

Last word on the mandatory P.S. goes to one of America's most accomplished fundraising copywriters, George Crankovic, senior writer at TrueSense, blogger at The Clued-In Copywriter. He recommends[3] that instead of a PS like this:

P.S. See your gift double in impact to save people from leprosy.

we can add some interest, maybe with something like this:

P.S. Act now to see your gift do twice as much good with matching funds. I've enclosed a stamped reply envelope for your convenience. What could be easier? Save these hurting people from leprosy. Please give now.

Then again, we can power up the P.S. with even more energy, maybe like this:

P.S. Did you know that men are twice as likely to get leprosy as women? Science can't explain why. But we do know that leprosy is completely curable—with your support. Please give now, and your generosity will:

- Double in impact with matching funds, doing twice as much good to save lives.
- Deliver the antibiotics that will cure suffering people of leprosy.
- Send doctors and nurses into poverty zones to treat and heal these hurting people.
- Demonstrate the cause of Christ at work in our world.
- And much more.

Bless these suffering people with your compassion and show God's love. Please give now to transform the lives that leprosy tries to destroy. I'm counting on you. Please give now.

That's pretty long—almost a whole new letter. But since the P.S. is so important, isn't it worth taking some space from the letter to make the P.S. stronger? It would be an interesting test.

P.S. Whatever you do, don't skip the P.S. on your fundraising letter!

~ George C.

3 Noted in *Future Fundraising Now*, March 23, 2017

CHAPTER 41

What are you writing today: acquisition, existing or lapsed?

You cannot write a successful appeal until you have one person clearly in mind: the recipient, the target audience, the person you're trying to speak with, the person you hope will help your cause.

Many charities—smaller, local ones especially—will try to get by, writing just one annual appeal and sending it to every mail box, whether the addressee knows the cause or not.

But successful one-size-fits-all letters are as rare as hen's teeth. I've met exactly two in my years.[1]

The majority of charity appeals serve one of the following purposes: (1) acquiring new donors[2]; (2) renewing annual gifts from current donors; (3) asking for additional gifts from current donors; and (4) re-acquiring so-called "lapsed" donors.

- You send **acquisition** appeals to people who've never made a gift to your cause. In the callous jargon of fundraising, you're trying to "acquire" them for your donor list.

- You send **renewal** appeals to people who *have* made a gift to your cause fairly recently; within, say, the last 18 months.

- You send **additional** appeals to current donors because they are your very best prospects. I was told that a public television station in the United States receives 1.3 gifts a year from the average donor. In other words, everyone gives once—and a third of those same donors give a second time, to some other appeal.

- You send **re-acquisition** appeals to people who once gave to your cause but for some reason stopped. If you're familiar with university fundraising, you've encountered conventions like LYBUNT (gave Last Year But Unfortunately Not

1 One, an annual appeal for a small-town public library appears on p. 147 of this chapter.

2 Or you might call them members or supporters. Whichever name you prefer, they are the people who commit the money and time to keep the charity healthy and sufficiently resourced to grow.

This) and SYBUNT (gave Some Year But Unfortunately Not This) to segment lapsed donors into even smaller sub-groups.

Howdy, strangers

Recognize that you send acquisition appeals to people who may have little-to-no real idea who you are or why you need their help.

Sure, people drive by your library every week . . . but do they know you're a charity? Sure, people graduate in the tens of thousands annually from state universities like yours . . . but do they know those same schools over the last 30 years have relied more and more on charity to compete and thrive?

The average for alumni giving to state universities in the United States is beggarly, for instance. Last time I looked, something like 13% of state U alums gave annually to their alma maters. Yet, elite private schools can see annual alumni giving as high as 60%.[3]

Never assume someone knows you and your needs. It's a dangerous assumption that leaves most of the money on the table. It's far safer (i.e., lucrative) to assume that all—including your volunteers, congregation, alumni, patients, the families of children you help, even your own board sometimes (sigh)—are strangers to your organization's fundraising needs.

When trying to acquire first-time donors, treat them as people with a great capacity for empathy and compassion. But assume they know nothing about your needs.

In an acquisition appeal, you'll want to answer questions like these:

1. Who are you?
2. What do you want from me?
3. Why should I trust you? Do you have results?
4. Why is this important to me?
5. What's the rush?
6. Will I feel better if I make the gift?

Renewal appeals go to active participants in the mission. Consider these people your "philanthropic family" or your "supporter family." Treat them as beloved colleagues. Don't be afraid to ask them often for their help.

---

3 Princeton University average between 2008 and 2011.

In a renewal appeal, you'll want to answer questions like these:

1. Are you grateful?
2. What was my last gift?
3. How did my contribution make a difference?
4. Is there still a need for more help?
5. Are you embracing me as family?

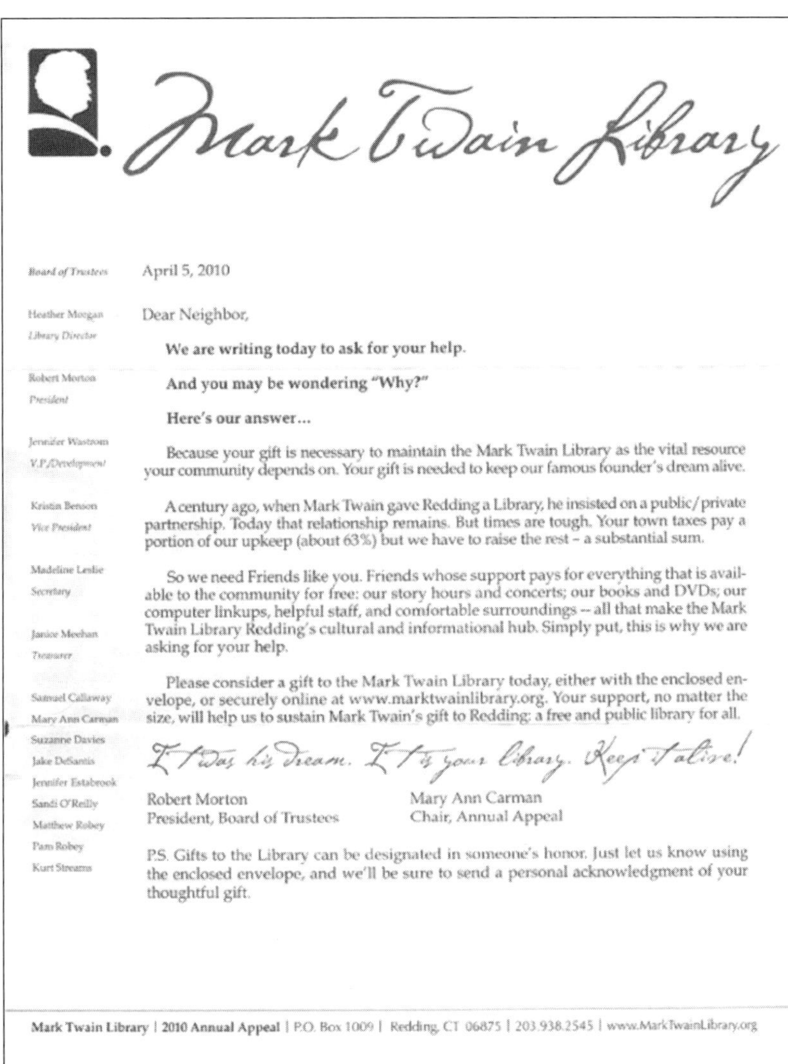

Mark Twain Library

April 5, 2010

Dear Neighbor,

We are writing today to ask for your help.

And you may be wondering "Why?"

Here's our answer...

Because your gift is necessary to maintain the Mark Twain Library as the vital resource your community depends on. Your gift is needed to keep our famous founder's dream alive.

A century ago, when Mark Twain gave Redding a Library, he insisted on a public/private partnership. Today that relationship remains. But times are tough. Your town taxes pay a portion of our upkeep (about 63%) but we have to raise the rest – a substantial sum.

So we need Friends like you. Friends whose support pays for everything that is available to the community for free: our story hours and concerts; our books and DVDs; our computer linkups, helpful staff, and comfortable surroundings -- all that make the Mark Twain Library Redding's cultural and informational hub. Simply put, this is why we are asking for your help.

Please consider a gift to the Mark Twain Library today, either with the enclosed envelope, or securely online at www.marktwainlibrary.org. Your support, no matter the size, will help us to sustain Mark Twain's gift to Redding: a free and public library for all.

It was his dream. It is your library. Keep it alive!

Robert Morton
President, Board of Trustees

Mary Ann Carman
Chair, Annual Appeal

P.S. Gifts to the Library can be designated in someone's honor. Just let us know using the enclosed envelope, and we'll be sure to send a personal acknowledgment of your thoughtful gift.

Mark Twain Library | **2010 Annual Appeal** | P.O. Box 1009 | Redding, CT 06875 | 203.938.2545 | www.MarkTwainLibrary.org

Jenn Wastrom was a board member when she penned this remarkably lucrative letter. She was not a professional copywriter. She had maybe three hours of workshop training in direct mail. And her letter broke at least two direct mail "rules": it bore two signatures and wasn't personalized beyond "Dear Neighbor." And yet this one-size-fits-all letter that told no story raised a stunning $55,926 in two months via a mailing that went to just 4,600 households in the small town of Redding, Connecticut.

CHAPTER 42

How often can you ask in a year?

In an "oh, heck, let's just see what happens" test, one North American charity sent out and monitored 21 individual direct mail asks . . . before they detected any real backlash.

Doesn't seem possible?

And yet . . . yeah, it is.

It's complicated

We were at the Nonprofit Storytelling Conference in Seattle, mid-November, 2014. The hall held a rare concentration of top experts. At a table near the stage sat Jeff Brooks, a senior copywriter at TrueSense, one of America's best direct mail firms.

I was speaking. A fundraiser in the audience asked a seemingly simple question: "How often can you ask in a year without losing donors?"

I'm not qualified to answer. I glance at Jeff. He flashes the number 20 with his fingers. *Really?* Me, clueless.

Just then a fundraiser grabs the mic. He describes a test he's done with his organization, to see what his donors' base tolerance for asking really is. In short: they mailed 21 solicitations in just one year before gifts tapered off completely.

Come on: is 21 *really* all that intrusive? It comes down to fewer than two solicitations per month.

During US presidential campaigns I'd get more than two emailed solicitations *per day* from candidates I supported. That's 60 solicitations a month per candidate. Yet I did not UNsubscribe.

Over-solicitation is not your real problem, is it?

Stand in awe of this shocking true-life maximum number of 21.

And at the very same time know that most charities—including yours—are likely nowhere close.

In answer to the basic question, "How many times a year should I mail my donors?" Canadian expert Alan Sharpe advises, "Mail at least eight times a year.

Mail at least four appeal letters and mail at least four newsletters (or donor cultivation, donor information type pieces)."[1]

Are you mailing that often? I hope so: frequency, telling the right people the same message over and over and over, is a basic secret to fundraising success.

It's funny, though

Paradoxically, avoidably, one reason so many first-time donors do not make a second gift[2] is *under*-, not over-, communication. Basically, because you're not in touch at all, these new donors forget about you or never form any kind of bond with you.

Don't be misled.

In focus groups, veteran donors complain long and loud about being over-solicited by their favorite charities. But if you watch their giving behavior, you will find that they don't stop giving as a result.

Fabienne, my French cousin-in-law, is a perfect example. She's a retired teacher, married with one adult son. She's got a big heart. She volunteers and gives to about two dozen charities a year, prompted by direct mail. She's given to some for decades.

And the ONLY thing she doesn't like about them and will sharply criticize is over-solicitation. "I give every year," she steams. "Why do they send me appeals all the time?" She sees it as wasteful. Her opinion, in sum: "Spend that money on the mission, not extra mailings!" Yet . . . despite this "appeal harassment" and a presumption of donor fatigue . . . Fabienne continues to give to the same charities year after year.

In November 2014, the CEO of Grizzard, Chip Grizzard, reported on some surprising test results. In the test, donors of $500 or more were allowed to limit the number of appeals they'd receive in the coming year. If they didn't specify otherwise, they'd receive 12 appeals. "Of the 500 in the group," Chip wrote, "186 [37%] wrote back and designated the specific mailings they wanted during the next 12-month mailing cycle. Interestingly, the most mailings anyone selected was three."

The end-of-year results surprised everyone. "The donors who received all 12 mailings gave 35% more than the ones [who'd limited their appeals]. What did the test sponsor learn? 'I learned that unless a major donor asks to limit his/her mailings, they should stay with the normal cultivation strategy. You never know when something will strike a donor's fancy. Each appeal is different.'"

---

1 Alan Sharpe, *Mail Superiority* (London, Ontario: Andrew Spencer Publishing, 2008): 228.

2 Data released by Blackbaud in 2014 showed that over three-quarters (76%) of first-time donors do not give a second time to the same charity.

Jeff Brooks commented, "There's an important lesson here: **Less mail, less giving.** That's true in nearly every situation. Including major donors. Never assume donors will give more or retain longer if they get less contact. It almost never works that way."

Don't over-react to complaints about over-solicitation. They're probably false alarms. And certainly don't listen to the timid amongst us who fret, "We'll drive off our donors if we ask too often." While it sounds reasonable, even considerate, the science says it's dead wrong. The correct view is "We'll leave a lot of money on the table if we don't ask often enough."

One last thing.

Since I've tripped over this peculiar misunderstanding more than once, let's be clear: when we talk about an "annual fund," the word "annual" has nothing to do with asking just once a year. It has only to do with what you're raising money for: your charity's *annual* operating expenses.

One cure for complaints about "over solicitation"? Choice.

Bearing in mind the results Chip Grizzard reported on, there is a countermeasure you can take that will fend off complaints about over-solicitation: send your first-time donors a little questionnaire that asks them about their "communications preferences."

The survey should ask these newcomers what they want to get from you (email, annual reports, special appeals, annual appeals) and how often.

This kind of courtesy up front can prove profitable down the road. Dr. Adrian Sargeant's research found that donors, when asked their "communications preferences," tended to stay with charities longer and make bigger average gifts.

"Offering donors a choice is key," he wrote in *Fundraising Principles and Practice*.[3] "When do you want to hear from us? What aspects of our work are you interested in? Would you like e-mail or regular mail? Are you interested in a newsletter or a once-a-year update? Would you like news but not to be asked for money?"

Dr. Sargeant offers as his best example the communications survey used by the Camphill community of nonprofits in the United Kingdom. It's printed on the back of every communication the charity sends out. The survey allows the donor to choose or change the frequency of newsletters. It allows the donor to continue getting information but halt all appeals. It even allows the donor to check this box: "I would prefer you NOT to write me again."

---

3 Adrian Sargeant and Jen Shang, *Fundraising Principles and Practice* (San Francisco: Jossey-Bass, 2010): [page number].

Crazy? Like a fox. As Dr. Sargeant points out, "Offering donors choice has been the foundation of Camphill's [fundraising] success." Jeff Brooks confirms the phenomenon:

> I've had the same results from this, and the really amazing thing is that you get better long-term value [LTV] from all the groups in this scenario:
>
> - Those who return the questionnaire and in some way ask for reduced communication.
> - Those who respond but don't limit you
> - That VAST majority (90%+) who don't respond at all
>
> All groups improve their LTV. The only group that doesn't is those who say "remove me from your list" (and that's a TINY group).

CHAPTER 43

How soon will we know our results?

In 2016, I asked two big-time direct mail fundraisers that question: "How soon will we know whether an appeal is working or not?"

Roger Craver said that, in the United States, a direct mail appeal sent third class to a *local* audience would see 50% of its returns in two to two and a half weeks. An appeal sent third class to a *national* audience would see 50% of its returns in four to six weeks.

If the appeal was sent first class, the local return rate remained the same, but the national return rate was slightly faster, at three to five weeks to reach 50%.

Jeff Brooks agreed, noting that "during November and December, count on everything being slower than normal, thanks to the holiday crush."

CHAPTER 44

The Domain Formula for print newsletters

Remember the donor communications mantra?

Ask. Thank. Report. Repeat.

Ask me for my help. Thank me for my help. Report back to me what was done with my help.

Asking seems obvious. Thanking seems obvious. But how do you go about reporting? What's the foolproof way to fulfill that obligation?

The best answer I know: mail to your donors a print newsletter built to the specifications of the Domain Formula.

"You mean an emailed newsletter, right?"

Sorry, no. I know email seems easier. Faster. Cheaper. Far more reasonable in a busy office. But, if you want to make money, print newsletters are the proven way to go.

In fact, these days you'll want to do both: print and email newsletters. Properly done, print will raise money, while email will help you stay in touch more frequently and nurture connections.

Testing, testing

Earlier in this book you read how the Nashville Rescue Mission makes $2+ million a year in donations *from its print newsletter alone*. What is their secret? The Mission adopted and adapted the Domain Formula, developed in the 1990s by Seattle's Domain Group.

How *did* Domain turn the common charity newsletter from a bit player into a money-making star? By taking nothing for granted. Domain tested basic questions:

- What's the ideal length for a newsletter?
- What kind of content should it carry?
- What should it look like?

They overturned a few industry assumptions along the way.

- Assumption #1: a self-mailer is just fine, thank you.
- Assumption #2: a newsletter is a PR tool. It's for telling the world about your organization and for educating the donor.
- Assumption #3: newsletters don't make money.

On the contrary, Domain's research revealed:

- Self-mailed newsletters produced lousy results. They will save you money up front . . . and lose you money on the back end.
- A charity newsletter is not a PR tool. It's a reporting device. It has to do just one thing to be effective: show how your donors' philanthropy is changing the world.
- A good charity newsletter can make overflowing buckets of money.

The original Domain Formula

- **Send four pages, in a standard format.** In the United States and Canada, the standard single-page format measures 8.5 x 11 inches. In the United Kindgom and other Commonwealth nations, the standard single-page format is taller and narrower: the A4. Whatever; it's just rectangles. What *is* important is this: you don't have to send your donors a big, thick production. Four pages of trenchant copy is fine. Sufficient. Enough. They will reward you for being blessedly brief.
- **Don't worry about how many inks you use.** Some hyper-cautious charities might wonder: "Will our donors think we're wasting money if we use color printing?" No. Research shows it's a non-issue. Full-color printing brings in gifts. One-color printing brings in gifts. Of course, if you ask the opinion of an 85-year-old donor who grew up when color printing was a luxury, before the advent of short-run, low-cost, digital printing via the Internet, she might say that full-color printing is a bit wasteful—but she'd still give. Don't overthink this.
- **Do NOT send a self-mailer. Send the newsletter in an envelope instead.** This is the one that trips up many charities. They want to save money on their newsletter, which they typically view as an expense with little-to-no measurable return on investment (ROI). The cheapest way to mail a newsletter is to shun the added expense of an envelope and use a self-mailing format instead. That's a mistake. Repeat tests by Domain conclusively showed that self-mailers do not produce good results. Gifts do not roll in. The same newsletter in an envelope, on the other hand, could produce lots of gifts. Why the difference? The best

guess at Domain was that self-mailed newsletters had "low perceived value," to use marketing jargon. Which is one way of saying that they mostly just got tossed in the trash unread.

- **On your newsletter's envelope, run a small amount of teaser copy** that says something like, *Dear wonderful human being, the latest issue of your donor newsletter enclosed.* (Or for certain specialized audiences: *The latest issue of your donor newsletter lies coiled inside like a cobra!*) A teaser that instantly tells recipients "this is not another request for money" will increase your open rate.
- **Send your newsletter exclusively to current donors.** Nonprofits have all sorts of formulas for mailing newsletters. Some send *only* to donors who make gifts above a certain level. Generally, this is a self-defeating policy, since loyal $10 annual donors are actually superb candidates for making charitable bequests, studies show. Some send to *everyone* including the mayor's office, every foundation they've ever met, plus your Crazy Aunt Nellie—just on general principles. "Couldn't hurt, right?" The shotgun approach is costly, though. Domain found that, for highest ROI, you should ONLY mail to current donors. Simple.
- **Include a reply envelope and a reply device.** Or an all-in-one reply envelope with integrated device. Does not matter. The envelope/device is there (1) to reinforce the idea that you need gifts, and (2) to give responsive donors a convenient way to return a gift check.

MY HELP FOR OUR NEIGHBORS IN NEED THIS SUMMER

Yes, Glenn, I know that our community's hungry, hurting, and homeless need me, so here's my help to meet the need in the summer weeks ahead of us. I'm enclosing:

[ ] $20.00 [ ] $__________to help as many as I can right now.

[ ] I'm also enclosing my "Camper Bunk Tag" to bless a needy child at summer camp!

NASHVILLE RESCUE MISSION

639 Lafayette Street | Nashville, TN 37203
615-312-1532

Make checks payable to
Nashville Rescue Mission.

To charge your gift, complete the information on the reverse side.

REMEMBER:
You can give your gift securely online today!
nashvillerescuemission.org

[ ] I have remembered Nashville Rescue Mission in my estate plans.

To stay connected and receive email updates provide your email address in the space below:

05-1607 225078

Dear Mr. and Mrs. Buckley,

Summer is just ahead and during those hot, difficult months, the need will only intensify for our most vulnerable neighbors. That's why I encourage you to remember how vital your gifts and prayers are to those we serve—together, we are helping save and change lives!

Please give $20.00 or more today to make a lifesaving difference for those who need you most, like you did with your gift of $20.00 in March.

Please also take a moment to sign and send the "Camper Bunk Tag" I've enclosed. It will mean so much to a child who is excited about the opportunity to experience a Christ-centered camp this summer.

NASHVILLE RESCUE MISSION 639 Lafayette Street, Nashville, TN 37203
www.nashvillerescuemission.org

- **Mail "as often as possible."** Success is no accident; it's built step by step. If one of your newsletters produces an eyebrow-lifting amount of donor revenue, then double the frequency of the newsletter. If it continues to produce large amounts of income, then increase your frequency again. Nashville Rescue Mission can send its newsletter monthly and make eye-popping amounts of money with every issue. But let's be honest. Most charities aren't ready for that kind of full-court press. Take baby steps. If you're sending your newsletter just once a year, that's an annual report. A three-times-a-year printed newsletter is subsistence living. A quarterly printed newsletter is probably the true bare minimum.
- **Focus on accomplishment reporting.** "Accomplishment reporting" was Domain's term for "telling your donors the good things you did with their money." *Accomplishment reporting* is what your donors need to hear—in fact, what they *crave* hearing. Skip this, and your newsletter will fail: a one-step checklist.

What Jeff Brooks learned later

As noted before, Jeff Brooks is one of America's top fundraising direct mail copywriters. He was also a key member of the Domain team that developed the newsletter formula in the 1990s. In 2012, he sent me a note mentioning a few additional things he'd learned in the years since. In Jeff's own words:

- Less than four pages has not done well. When we've tested a single-sheet newsletter (8.5x11 or 8.5x14 inches) it has meaningfully underperformed a typical 4-page format. Cheaper, but the loss in revenue more than undercuts the production savings.
- A different format that has done well is this: four pages plus a 3-inch "flap." The entire form is 11x20 instead of 11x17 inches; the flap folds in over page 3. Allows for a little more content, and the cost difference is very little.
- Full color. When tested against two-color, four-color usually at least pays for itself. Full color seems to have the most positive impact for larger national organizations. It's worth testing, but not an automatic winner for everyone. (The cost difference between 2 and 4 color has shrunk; very often nowadays 2-color printing is done on 4-color presses; adding the other two colors adds very little expense.)
- Reply device printed in the newsletter as well as on the reply envelope. This usually gives a meaningful boost to response. Organizations get very few of these printed reply devices back, but they seem to have the function of driving more people to the separate RD that's in the envelope.
- "Newsletter enclosed" is the best teaser.
- You CAN ask in a newsletter. The newsletters that have appeals built into them, such as a lead story about some problem or opportunity that needs donor support, get the strongest response.
- Newsletters are not equally effective for all organizations. They work better for local orgs than national ones. They generally work better for religious orgs than non-religious. Organizations that have had newsletters for a while can usually improve response to newsletters and add more issues to the calendar. If you have no newsletter now, do 3 or 4 in the coming year. If they work, add more issues each year.
- 13 seems to be too many. We had a client that did a newsletter every month, and newsletters generally did better than appeal letters. So we added a 13th

issue (in place of an appeal in the thick of the year-end season). That 13th did worse than most appeals.

- Try a personalized newsletter. Use lasering or digital printing to get the donor's name into headlines and other content. This works well, and pays for itself (though we have the feeling that it would get less effective if used a lot). Imagine the power of this headline: "Mr. and Mrs. Example helped hungry people this summer!"

P.S.

Let's give the last word to Jeff Schreifels, another Domain alumnus. He wrote me in 2012, about a client of his: "They too embraced the 'Domain formula' about 8 years ago. They have 350,000 donors. They send 12 donor-focused newsletters per year, along with 12–13 appeal letters and each newsletter brings in over $1MM in revenue! I'm not kidding. The newsletter actually brings in more revenue than their appeals. Those newsletters consistently bring in over a 4.5 to 5 to 1 ROI. Never have seen anything like it."

CHAPTER 45

Content for newsletters

Jeff Brooks recommends four types of content for donor newsletters. This content suits both print and digital formats:

- **Stories (not statistics) that take readers to the front lines.**

  Stories related to the mission. Stories that also take time to note the donor's importance in the story, and note it in the big type, not the small.

  Newsletter stories, for instance, headlined as this one was for Providence Hospice of Seattle Foundation: "Hospice gives a beloved grandma the gift of dying at home. Your gifts are helping a grieving granddaughter with the loss of her 'second mom.'"

  These kinds of stories "take donors on a journey." That's one of Adrian Sargeant's Seven Principles of Donor Loyalty; in other words, a reason why donors stick with a charity rather than soon flee (as most do).

  Show your donors intriguing, soulful, surprising things they've never seen before. Reawaken their empathy in every issue.

- **Stories about donors "just like you."** There is in psychology something called "social proof." It's also known as the "bandwagon effect." We model some of our behavior on things we see others do. If someone we admire acts a certain way, we might want to act that way as well.

  "Social proof" helps explain why celebrities can be useful in advocacy and fundraising. John Wayne, famously, massively reduced littering in Texas by saying he was against it. But celebrities are the least of social proof.

  We look to those we consider peers for social clues. "What do people like me do?"

  If, for instance, I read a story in my charity newsletter about a donor who's joined the legacy society by putting a gift in *her* will, then I might—just might—imagine doing the same thing the next time I update *my* will. After all, we're both donors to the same cause. We're in the same tribe. We're socio-economic peers. *She's like me.*

It's tricky, though. It's easy to break the spell. It's easy to make people feel like outsiders not insiders. If all you report in your donor newsletter are big gifts from major donors, will small donors easily identify? Unlikely. They'll feel like cast-outs. Very likely they'll conclude: "Well, that's not me. I don't have that kind of money."

In the case of charitable bequests, that would be an unfortunate conclusion, since volumes of data show that most charitable bequests in North America come from the middle class, not the wealthy.[1]

- **People served saying thanks.** "Bridget has a special message for you" reads the headline over one Dana-Farber donor newsletter story. In it, survivor Bridget Spence thanks donors for making possible a breakthrough program aimed especially at young women with breast cancer. Do you have an online video of kids saying thanks, as one of my favorite charities, Nyaka School,[2] has? Promote that video loud and clear in your print and digital newsletters, and on Facebook and other social media. There are truths that should always be seen incised as caps in granite, and this is one: DONORS WILL NEVER TIRE OF HEARING YOU THANK THEM.

- **Offers that encourage deeper involvement.** Of any kind; it doesn't matter.

  This is another of professor Adrian Sargeant's Seven Principles of Donor Loyalty. This one's called "multiple engagements." Meaning? If your donor does more than just make gifts to your charity, that donor will probably yield a higher lifetime value (LTV).

  Ideally, you want your donors to say, "I'm in. What else can I do?"

  - **Actions like volunteering:** "Mentor. There's a young, inexperienced brain just waiting for your older, more experienced one to come along and show her how!"

  - **Actions like advocacy:** "Please sign this petition before we dig this particular policy hole any deeper!"

---

1 "[T]here is no correlation between either income or wealth with the likelihood of giving by bequest . . . the average bequest, now about $35,000 in the US, typically comes from the estate of a retired woman who either has no living children, or feels they've got enough money of their own." Mal Warwick quoting Robert F. Sharpe, Jr., circa 2005.

2 For AIDS orphans in Uganda.

- **Actions like attending events:** "You're invited to the most important environmental event in Alabama history!"
- **Actions like charitable bequests:** "This will likely be the most important gift you ever make."

Charities? Offer a full spectrum of actions . . . for the introverted to the extroverted . . . from the poor as church mice to the obscenely wealthy.

"Deeper involvement" is not about the few. "Deeper involvement" hopes to activate as many as possible, to light up as much of your donor pyramid as possible, base to peak. It is not exclusive. It's intentionally inclusive.

CHAPTER 46

Big type matters most

Most online "readers" in fact read very little, as Slate reported in 2013 (that was then; it's only getting worse). Many do not scroll. Most read just 50% of an article (about four typical paragraphs). And pictures hog most of the available attention, the research shows.

None of this is news to communications pros, of course. Getting people to read in depth was always tough, as the Poynter newspaper research showed. Looking quickly at the big splashes of ink (or pixels) and moving on is the default.

Resistance is futile.

I assume that most readers do an initial speedy skim of a publication—case, annual report, donor newsletter, brochure, website . . . *before* they dig in any deeper . . . *if* they dig in at all.

In self-defense, I put no special eggs in the small-type basket. Any message I want people to get I put in the big type: the headlines and other high-visibility, short-form writing such as eyebrows, decks, captions and pull quotes. They do most of the work.

How a simple headline change doubled gift income

It takes about the same time to write a strong headline as a weak one. What differs is the impact on your income.

Weak headlines leave money on the table because donors and prospects remain uninformed as well as unmoved. Faint-hearted headlines do not spur gifts. Strong-hearted headlines bring in far more money.

I know one national advocacy group that changed the headlines in its donor newsletter—and as a result doubled their gift income between one issue and the next. But that's not all: the average size of the newsletter-generated gifts was surprisingly large, almost *double* the average gift size from the organization's appeal letters.

This was a typical front-page headline from their old newsletter: "From the Executive Director." And that's all. Same thing, issue after issue: From the Executive Director. (And they called it a newsletter.)

This was the lucrative front-page headline from the new, improved newsletter: "Senior Republican Wants to Draft You in the War on Drugs." Now, that's more like it. Nobody wants bland headlines from an advocacy organization. You're in a fight!

Well-written headlines can scream like fire alarms in the minds of those predisposed to care about your mission.

Here's the test

Cover or delete the articles in your next case, annual report or donor newsletter. Leave just the headlines and the other bigger type visible.

Does your piece still make sense?

Is the big type alone convincing?

Are you still getting your key points across in the big type about your love of donors and your need for their ongoing help?

If not, do your organization's fortunes a favor and rewrite the headlines.

Breakthroughs you've helped make happen

Crowdsourced drug promotes "memory loss" in cancer cells

Revolutionary research leads to revolutionary discoveries

What if it were possible to make cancer cells "forget" their deadly mission and instead turn into white blood cells or other harmless structures?

That is the innovative idea behind some amazing

Lives you've touched

Survivors are "Living Proof" cancer can be beaten

Medical treatment is only a part of what your support provides for people with cancer

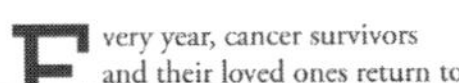

Every year, cancer survivors and their loved ones return to

An "eyebrow" in journalism is a short line of type above the headline. Its purpose is to hook the skimming reader. Here, a Dana-Farber donor newsletter uses eyebrows effectively to frame its stories with high-visibility donor-centricity. Eyebrows are small but powerful.

Planned Parenthood launches chic new condom brand

- Released for Valentine's Day under the trade name Proper Attire™
- New "fashion statement" condoms come in choice of styles
- Waiting for a man to provide the condom? That's so "last season," says PPFA

PLANNED PARENTHOOD HAS SOMETHING NEW to offer women who are sexually active, stylish, and want to protect their health: a line of attractively packaged condoms called *Proper Attire,*™ FDA-approved and rigorously tested for quality assurance. The new condom brand has a remind-your-man subtitle: *Required for Entry.*™

"From the chic packaging to the playful brand name," says PPFA, "we've made sure that women will feel confident buying and using Proper Attire condoms. Old stereotypes about who should buy condoms are so 'last season.' Nowadays, women and men both understand how important it is to use protection every time you have sex."

Proper Attire condoms are available at PPRI's clinic and Express, in several styles: basic (plain lubricated), XL, dots (studded), and colored.

A "deck" in journalism is a "subordinate head that follows a newspaper's main headline," says Barbara G. Ellis, author of *The Copy-Editing and Headline Handbook*. A headline and its deck act as one unit, to be read at one glance. In this article from a donor newsletter for a Planned Parenthood affiliate, the headline and a three-item bulleted deck tell the full story of a new product being introduced. The photo serves to drag the eye down and across the headline and deck. The article adds more information. But you didn't have to read it to get the key points: the headline and deck clarified them quickly and early.

One last pep rally

The weird, uncomfortable blessing of fundraising

by Jeff Brooks

I was in Uganda, gathering stories on behalf of a client. At that time, Uganda was Ground Zero of the AIDS epidemic. The disease had devastated parts of the country, killing nearly all adults under 60. The tranquil beauty of the countryside gave the impression of the richness of life. The reality was a place as ruined as if there'd been a nuclear holocaust.

I was visiting some of the hardest-hit communities. We saw no adult men or women, other than white-haired elderly ones—but there were children everywhere.

Most of my interviews were with older women. They'd ended up caring for their grandchildren after their own children died of AIDS. They typically had a dozen or more grandchildren in their care, all orphans, all with no source of care but grandma—who struggled to feed them all.

In one especially devastated community, an old woman approached me and asked if I was a priest. I told her I was not.

"So minister," she said, then hurried away. I learned later that the community experience was that the only white people who visited them were clergy. And if I wasn't a priest, I must be the next best thing, a minister.

A few minutes later, the old woman returned. She was holding a baby. She motioned me to follow her. We walked a few yards, pushing through a thick tropical forest until we emerged into a clearing the size of my dining room. The ground was a square of black soil, raked into steep furrows.

"Reverend bless," the old woman said, motioning at the ground.

She wanted me to bless the garden plot. To invoke God's power on the urgently needed crop.

And then, before I could even start to wonder how you bless a garden, she thrust the baby into my arms. "Bless baby," she said.

I stood there at the edge of the garden plot, sleeping baby in my arms, and wondered what to do. I felt profoundly uncomfortable, terribly inadequate; I wanted to beg off, to explain how I was the wrong guy, to get away.

Fortunately, an insight came to me: I had *no choice* but to go through with the blessing they sought. I needed to figure it out and just get on with it.

My discomfort was nothing compared to their need for blessings. If I'd refused, it would have been merely an awkward extrication from an awkward situation—to me. To them, it would have been a crushing disappointment with potentially fatal repercussions. *What sort of clergyman would do that to them?* Or, as I asked myself, *What sort of human being would do that to them?*

I learned that day that *sometimes the role is bigger than the person playing it.* That sometimes doing the necessary thing can be seriously uncomfortable—but that is no reason back out.

This issue comes up in my work quite often in the form of a nonprofit leader who balks at signing a fundraising message he or she doesn't like.

The less experienced ones say, "This is just dumb. It'll never work. I know that because I wouldn't respond to it."

The more experienced ones say, "I realize this is how you motivate donors to give. But I don't talk this way! It makes me uncomfortable."

The true leaders (experienced or not) say, "I don't understand this, but I'm willing to sign if that's what it takes to get people to fund our cause."

The real leaders get it—a lot quicker than I did: sometimes you have to fake it and bless the baby and the garden. This may not be why you showed up to do the job, and you may feel unequipped to do it—it may seem over-the-top weird. But a role has been given you, and you need to take it.

I don't know if my blessings in Uganda that day had any efficacy on the garden. Or the baby. No doubt I got it wrong, but to this day I cherish the memory. It was one of those rare moments when the divine gets mixed up in normal life and leaves you changed. I still think about that baby sometimes. He'd be a young man by now. I hope he's having a good, productive, joyful life.

Life is that way. There are times you have to push aside your sense of who you are and what you're about in order to perform the role that you've been placed in.

So play the role; write the letter you think you'd never respond to. Or sign that letter. That's how you participate in the strange mechanisms of the world. It's how you transform the world around you. And yourself.

To every new fundraiser . . .

"The struggle for justice is a marathon, not a sprint. And the biggest contribution that any one of us can make is maintaining a lifetime of involvement until we win those struggles."

—Kumi Naidoo, former Greenpeace International Executive Director; via Reinier Spruit, 101Fundraising blog

- Successful fundraising is hard work.

  Even *unsuccessful* fundraising is hard work.

  There are no quick answers, as you already know or will discover. Superheroes will not appear, to fill in your fundraising blanks. There are no quick answers. Don't waste your time trying to duplicate gimmicks like the Ice Bucket Challenge. Long before you hear about these "fresh" ideas, they are headed for oblivion and some cheesy game show called, "Remember When?"

- Fundraising is the hope business. You need believers.

  "Does it have to be this bad?" the potential donor whispered. *(This is what a true believer sounds like.)*

  "No!" the fundraiser assured her. "There is *real* hope . . . if we have your help. Will you join us, just to see? You don't have to stay. But please give us a try."[1]

- Without fundraisers, the work of most worthy causes—big and small, from human service to medical research to the arts—would, in fact, end. Just stop.

We live in a suffering world . . . despite abundant comforts here in the developed world, where I received my education, my abundant and under-appreciated privilege and now reside.

I seek the safety and predictability of those comforts. But my eyes and ears are open: *we live in a suffering world.*

It's gruesome. It makes you want to vomit and tear your hair. Yet, if you have

1 Some groups—in the arts maybe—might object that they're not "in the hope business." E.g., "We don't have sick kids!" I think "selling hope" *does* apply to you, and you need to figure out how.

some extra cash, you can do something about it, with your gifts to various charities over the years.

One qualified observer estimates there are now more than 10 million registered nonprofit organizations around the planet, with 1.8 million tax-exempt organizations in the United States alone.

That's how big the hurt is.

Perspective is what changes you

Astronaut Mike Massimino wrote, "Leaving the planet is unlike anything else . . . you realize that we're very lucky, that we're living in a paradise."

Mike might have also said, "Most of us are barely subsisting in the midst of what *could be* a paradise." At least 80% of humanity lives on less than $10 a day. Ninety-eight out of 100 people around the world today are poor. Poor, powerless, vulnerable in ways we can hardly imagine to disease, corruption, lack of education.

Most nonprofits exist because somewhere a small group of people—caring, pained people—learned about some form of horrific suffering and could not abide standing by any longer, pretending to be aloof.

They were sad. They were furious. They had drive. They would not quit. They tattooed a solemn purpose on their souls: "Somebody's got to do something about this. Looks like it's up to us. Who among you will help?"

Good luck, my dear fundraiser. You're already a hero for trying. Knowledge is your friend. Ignorance is your enemy. And so you have this book in your hand. It's armor of a sort.

Acknowledgments

Easily a thousand mentors have tramped through my head. I am unspeakably, immeasurably grateful. It is one of the reasons I love the nonprofit world: it is gracious and giving and people tell you how they do things. Here are *just those* mentioned or behind the scenes in this particular book (and if I've stupidly omitted your name, please do not be offended; I am grateful to you and reverent):

AFP
Agents of Good
The Agitator
AHP
AIGA
Tobin Aldrich
Angel Aloma
American Marketing Association
Ron Arena
Ask Direct (Ireland)
Audubon
Australia for Dolphins
Antoine Bechara
Tom Belford
The Benefactor Group
Bishop Ward High School
Blackbaud
Bloomerang
Bluefrog (UK)
Tim Bostic
Bow Valley College
Pat Bradley
John Briel
Michelle Brinson
Andrew Brommel
Jeff Brooks
Wendy Brovold
Warren Buffett
Ron Burke
Ken Burnett
Marie Burnett
Ken Burns
Donald B. Calne
Campbell & Company
Camphill
CASE
Denisa Casement
Cause & Effect
Christian Fundraising Consultancy
The Chronicle of Philanthropy
Robert B. Cialdini
Tina Cincotti
Alan Clayton
Maggie Cohn
Sandie Collette
Jeff Comfort
David Cooper
George Crankovic
Roger Craver
Crisis Aid International
Lisa Cron
Dana-Farber
Julie Decker
Domain Group (times infinity)
DonorDigital
Tony Elischer (fundraising misses you so much!)
Leah Eustace
Rudolf Flesch
Food for the Poor
Henry Ford
Friends of the Mississippi River
Fundraising Effectiveness Project
Joe Garecht
Tony Geoghegan
Gettysburg Foundation
Gayle Gifford
Seth Godin (bless you)
Good Works (Canada)
Howard Luck Gossage
Jonathon Grapsas
Fraser Green
Rory Green
Sheena Greer
Chip Grizzard
Pam Grow
Hampton Roads Community Foundation
Ann Hale

Sally Kirby Hartman
Chip & Dan Heath
Heifer Project International
Steve Herlich
Fred Hollows Foundation
Andrea Hopkins
Hospital for Sick Children in Toronto
Housing Works of RI
Houston Grand Opera
Huntington Society of Canada
Jerry Huntsinger
IABC
IFC
Simone Joyaux
Daniel Kahneman
Dean Karlan
J. Peter Kincaid
Joseph LeDoux
John Lepp
Richard C. Levin
Barb Levy
Stuart Levy
Beth Ann Locke
Lollypop Farm
Tony London
Chuck Longfield
David Love
Jay Love
Jen Love
Ian MacQuillin
Hal Malchow
Guy Mallabone
Marts & Lundy
Masterworks (blog)
McConkey Johnston International UK
Ruth McDonald
Mike McKenna
Harvey McKinnon (Canada)
Merchants Quay Ireland
Kristine Merz
John C. Meyers
Gwen Moss
Nashville Rescue Mission
National History Day
The Nature Conservancy
Mark Neigh
Damian O'Broin
David Ogilvy
One in Four
Ontario Nature
Orange Square Design
Oxfam
Jerry Panas (Jerold Panas Linzy & Partners)
Pareto (Australia)
Jill Pfitzenmayer
Mark Phillips
Stephen Pidgeon
Planned Parenthood
Poynter Institute
Providence Hospice of Seattle Foundation
Richard Radcliffe
Saint Louis Zoo
Adrian Salmon
Adrian Sargeant
Lisa Sargent
Patti Saunders
Jeff Schreifels
Science Daily
Steven Screen
Jen Shang
Jim Shapiro
Alan Sharpe
Robert F. Sharpe, Jr.
Steven Shattuck
Paul Slovic
George Smith
SOFII.org
Soi Dog Foundation
Solar Youth
David Solie
Special Olympics
George Stanois
Christiana Stergiou
Joseph Sugarman
Tangible (UK)
Target Analytic Group
Target Direct (UK)
Stephen Thomas (Canada)
Sean Triner
TrueSense (US)
Urban Institute
Nick Ut
Jose van Herpt
Julie Varee
Siegfried Vögele
Erica Waasdorp
Keith and Rosmarie Waldrop
Mal Warwick
Jenn Wastrom
Ryan West
Roger Williams Park Zoo
Wood River Land Trust
Cathie Wright
Yale Tomorrow
Jen Yuan
Paul J. Zak
Tammy Zonker

About the Author

Tom Ahern could walk into any bar in the fundraising world... and someone would buy him a drink.

He is considered one of the world's top authorities on how to make donor communications more profitable. He specializes in applying the discoveries of psychology and neuroscience to the day-to-day business of inspiring and retaining donors.

He is the author of four previous books on donor communications, all well received. Each year, he delivers dozens of workshops and webinars. Outside North America, he's spoken at the IFC in the Netherlands; several times in Australia and New Zealand; in Belgium, Italy, and Slovakia.

His recent clients for cases, direct mail, newsletters and training include Carnegie Library of Pittsburgh, Catholic Relief Services, Houston Grand Opera, the Museum of Flight (Seattle), National Parks Conservation Association, Princeton University, Save the Children, Sharp HealthCare and other major hospital systems, United Way of Anchorage, University of Chicago, Volunteers of America; as well as many smaller and local nonprofits. He collaborates with Prof. Adrian Sargeant and psychologist Jen Shang on prototyping innovative direct mail packages for PBS TV.

Tom Ahern has been an award-winning journalist, for articles on health and social justice. As a "message strategist," he's won three prestigious international IABC Gold Quill awards, all for nonprofit communications campaigns that achieved unusual success.

He graduated from Brown University with a BA and MA in English. He completed his Certificate of Advertising Art from the Rhode Island School of Design. His offices are in Rhode Island and France.

Of Related Interest

Making Money with Donor Newsletters

Tom Ahern, 166 pp., $24.95.

Making Money with Donor Newsletters will help you transform your current newsletter into a money machine—some charities that have followed this advice have improved income by 1,000 percent! More importantly it will guide you in transforming your organization from a ho-hum "corporate focused" entity into a distinctive and thriving "donor-focused" powerhouse.

Seeing Through a Donor's Eyes

Tom Ahern, 167 pp., $24.95.

Successful websites, annual reports, donor acquisition programs, email, direct mail, and, yes, capital campaigns too, all have one thing in common: behind each stands a well-reasoned, emotionally satisfying case for support. Regularly reviewing your case is due diligence in a well-managed fundraising office. And it doesn't have to be a laborious project. Answer a few questions and you're done. Of course, if your office is launching a big-bucks campaign, the step-by-step process revealed in this book guarantees that you will tell a persuasive, sharply focused story, even when you have a hundred moving parts.

The Fundraiser's Guide to Irresistible Communications

Jeff Brooks, 143 pp., $24.95.

Here it is: an easy to read and spritely book that reveals what really works in fundraising. Not academic theory or wishful thinking, but ways to communicate that are proven to motivate donors to give generously, wholeheartedly, and repeatedly. Drawing from decades of in-the-trenches experience, Jeff Brooks, one of America's top fundraising writers, takes you on a step-by-step tour of the unique strategies, writing style, and design techniques of irresistible fundraising messages.

How to Turn Your Words into Money

Jeff Brooks, 174 pp., $24.95

Are you ready to write your most effective fundraising message ever? One that touches donors' hearts, connects with their passions, and inspires them to give? Here's the book to help you do it. Jeff Brooks, one of America's top fundraising writers, pulls back the curtain on the counterintuitive world of fundraising to reveal, among other things, the one sentence top writers always use to start every project; the easy revision that will improve your writing nearly every time; the tested truth about making donors feel guilty; how the pros tell powerful stories even when they can't find the right story; and a proven template for a sure-fire, never-fail fundraising letter.

Copies of this and other books from the publisher are available at discount when purchased in quantity for boards of directors or staff. Call 508-359-0019 or visit www.emersonandchurch.com.

15 Brook Street—Medfield, MA 02052
Tel. 508-359-0019
www.emersonandchurch.com